Someone Is Buying the Zoo

Balancing Organization and Employee Needs
in Mergers and Acquisitions

CHARLOTTE FRAMPTON
CYNTHIA SURRISI
CAROLYN GALLAGHER

mollyockett press

st. paul

Copy, production editor: Ellen B. Green
Cover illustration: Dan Woychick
Design, computer keyline: Ellen B. Green
Printing: Sexton Printing, Inc.

© 1991 by Mollyockett Press, 275 Cimarron Road, St. Paul, MN 55124. All rights reserved.

Library of Congress Catalog Card Number: 90-92146

ISBN: 0-9628090-0-4

Manufactured in the United States of America

10 9 8 7 6 5 4 3 2 1

Contents

Foreword	vi
Preface & Acknowledgments	viii
Someone Is Buying the Zoo	
Chapter 1	1
Chapter 2	11
Chapter 3	29
Chapter 4	45
Chapter 5	55
Chapter 6	69
Chapter 7	84
Study Questions (by chapter)	96
The Dynamics of Corporate Culture	101
Breaking the "Us vs. Them" Barrier	106
The Human Process of Change	111
Suggestions	116
Bibliography	121

Foreword

Most of us find ourselves muttering from time to time that "this place is turning into a real zoo." What we mean is that things are in a mess and people are beginning to behave like animals. As bad as that state of affairs might be, it is only a mild version of the chaos that occurs when animals begin to act like humans—even when they start out as very happy animals.

Acquisitions and mergers are the organizational counterpart of marriage, where two humans bring their own family background to the party and where issues of contention often boil down to matters of dominance, control, and the lesser sides of the human spirit. The fact that acquisitions are so common and that they deal with the most fundamental aspects of human nature makes a compelling case for passing laws forbidding them as potentially injurious to the human race. Territory, identity, customs, habits, security, loss, aging, stress, and uncertainty are only the beginning of a list of concepts thrown up for grabs in the process of acquisition.

Our rationalizations for engaging in the process of acquisition—building a competitive advantage, making a healthy return on investments, providing what the public wants and "needs" and the means to make a living—make good reading. For obvious reasons, however, we don't find a lot of documentation about the weird goings-on in real companies undergoing the peculiar processes of acquisition.

This fictional description of the transition of Happy Valley Zoo to Zoolandia Theme Park Number 46 allows us to laugh at ourselves and our foibles as we screw things up under the guise of making progress, doing good, or simply trying to prepare for an uncertain future Whatever one's attitude about unions, for instance, it becomes clear we had to invent them as part of organizational culture. Whether unions already exist in our companies or we simply find people (workers or management) seriously considering banding together, the concept of unions moves to the forefront in the process of one company being acquired by another.

Through the use of thinly disguised animal characters, the authors of *Someone Is Buying the Zoo* provide a reasonably painless way to think about issues that are predictable but easy to forget as we consider whether to enter into the acquisition process. They show us that the difficulties of acquisition are more likely to be painfully obvious than deceptively obscure. Their work makes it easy to recognize other areas, too, in which we become involved without full awareness of the consequences. Through their storytelling we are shown the potential of breaking through our Saran Wrap® of denial and paying attention to the human factors affected by change in our organizations.

There is probably nothing inherently evil about making acquisitions, but it is definitely criminal to enter into the process without careful consideration of the potential for chaos, damage, and loss of the things we most wish to preserve. Reading these pages, I became more and more able to add to its list of "horribles and awfuls." This catalytic function is probably the most important contribution this book makes to our understanding of what it means to take seriously the process of implementing organization change. It may even help keep us from turning our organizations into zoos.

—CHARLES SEASHORE

Charles Seashore, Ph.D., a Washington, D.C., psychologist, is on the faculty of institutions including the Fielding Institute in Santa Barbara, California, the American University in Washington, D.C., Johns Hopkins University in Baltimore, Maryland, and the NTL Institute in Arlington, Virginia.

Preface & Acknowledgments

The 1980s were a decade of corporate consolidation in the form of mergers and acquisitions, a phenomenon that permanently altered the business community and employee perceptions regarding careers and job security. This trend continues in the 1990s as organizations expand for survival in a competitive global economy. No matter what the reason for consolidating, certain dynamics almost always occur in the process.

Mergers and acquisitions are specific types of corporate consolidations; their differences are in the legal domain and not relevant to this discussion. The impacts of the two processes upon the human element, however, are the same and to the point of this book. Because the story is about an acquisition, we use that term exclusively. Whatever its name, the prospect of the process of consolidation is viewed by employees of the merging companies as frightening and dangerous even when acquisition is the only avenue for corporate survival. Acquisition means drastic and sustained change.

In his book *Change Agents,* Manuel London introduces what he calls the "merger syndrome," its elements including internal battles over turf and job assignments, withheld communications fostering rumors, inaction, reduced productivity, more decline caused by uncertainty, and increased importance placed on self-interest rather than teamwork. London states that "overall, mergers lower employees commitment to the organization. Corporate goals become obscure and there is the perception of a weakened sense of direction. The best performers are likely to leave the company." Organizations wishing to survive must address the human issues associated with change especially during such major upheaval.

Someone Is Buying the Zoo takes the reader through the merging of two cultures, those of a worldwide conglomerate and a small family-owned zoo. As you read, consider the impact of the acquisition, the reaction of the characters, and how this acquisition could have been managed to avoid the merger syndrome. Following the narrative are end-of-chapter discussion questions providing an opportunity to assess the dynamics of the acquisition as it progresses. Related articles and acquisition management suggestions will help you identify effective approaches to acquisition management.

This book is intended, however, not to give a prescription for change but rather to provide opportunities for exploring options and to present information that deepens understanding of the human dynamics of the acquisitions process. Taking full responsibility for its contents, we thank Gene Frampton, Chuck Hanebuth, Laura Nichols, Charles Seashore, Jo Lowery, Patrick Brennaman, Sujata, and Kaje for their support and encouragement of this enterprise.

—CHARLOTTE FRAMPTON
—CYNTHIA SURRISI
—CAROLYN GALLAGHER

1

Ewald Elephant, known as Colonel to the animals, was president of Happy Valley, a little midwestern zoo. On this warm January afternoon, Colonel could see mothers and children strolling along the tree-lined walkways from the office window that gave him a view of the entire zoo.

Colonel was getting up in years and so was the zoo. It was looking frayed around the edges, getting terribly out of date. Colonel needed to find someone to take over the zoo, to lift the burden of responsibility—someone who had enough energy to undertake a major renovation.

Just two weeks earlier he had talked with his nephew, Elliott, a bright and ambitious young elephant who had worked his way up to president of the Theme Park Division of Zoolandia International. Colonel didn't mention it, but Elliott sensed Colonel's dilemma and in a flash invited Colonel to New York to talk about a purchase.

Elliott and his staff had treated Colonel with respect. Zoolandia would send its Tiger Team to Happy Valley Zoo to check out the feasibility of converting it to a Zoolandia theme park.

"Now I'm not promising anything, Ewald. Zoolandia has very strict standards about theme parks, and very few zoos are prime candidates for conversion," Elliott cautioned. And he gave Colonel instructions about the Tiger Team visit: To keep rumors to a minimum, the animals should be told the Tiger Team was working on a national research project.

When Colonel returned from New York, he didn't waste time before informing his staff of the impending visit. He called a meeting in the board room adjacent to his office.

"We've received a great honor here at Happy Valley, one that makes me very proud," Colonel paused for effect. "A distinguished group of zoological experts is visiting us to learn about our operations. Apparently they are very impressed with our zoo. I'd like you to show them our famous Happy Valley hospitality."

"Where're they from?" Ben Bear, vice president of Maintenance, spoke up.

"They're from Zoolandia. My nephew Elliott and I made arrangements for the visit while I was in New York last week. It's a real honor. I'm proud, mighty proud." Colonel looked around the room and smiled. No one returned his smile.

"Look here," Colonel began again. "We're going to be part of a national study, and we have a lot here that we can be proud of. What seems to be the problem?"

"I'll tell you what my problem is. I'm trying to get my repairs done while business is slow. I don't have time for a bunch of airheads asking dumb questions." Ben Bear was irritated.

"I'm in the middle of budget runs. Researchers don't care about budget runs. They can skip my department," Luke Shark chimed in.

"What's to see here?" Carl Crocodile spoke up. "Compared to Zoolandia, this place is archaic. There must be some other reason for their visit."

Several other staff members grunted assent. Colonel stood, towering over the table.

"I'm disappointed. I thought you'd be as excited as I am." Colonel glared around the room. "I expect you to be more gracious to the researchers than you've been to me today."

Then he passed out a memo. "See to it that every employee in your department gets this memo before the team arrives. I want everyone prepared. That's all." Colonel looked at each member before he strode from the room.

• • •

Happy Valley was a small zoo. Most of the animals had spent their entire lives there. As in any family, everyone knew when the head of the house was acting strange. The word went out: Colonel wasn't himself. He had yelled at his staff over a research team visit. Strange, they all said.

During the afternoon coffee break, a group of employees gathered at the concession stand. The chickens who worked there were quiet as Rodney Rooster, their supervisor, inventoried the red-and-white-striped popcorn bags.

When Rodney finished counting and headed for the food production building, the chickens began to talk. The concession stand was the

Happy Valley Zoo
INTEROFFICE MEMO

DATE: January 15
TO: Happy Valley Zoo Employees
FROM: Ewald J. Elephant, President
SUBJECT: Zoolandia Research

Representatives of the Zoolandia International, Theme Park Division, will be visiting our facilities this week, and talking with management and support personnel about our operations. We have been in the zoo game a long time, and our expertise and maturity can be of benefit to the National Zoo Study Team.

I expect all employees to cooperate fully with the study team during its brief stay. Thank you.

Zoolandia Representatives:
Mike Tiger, Leader
Ted Tiger, Maintenance Analyst
Archibald Tiger, Financial Analyst
Edwin Tiger, Operations Analyst
Liz Lioness, Animal Resource Analyst

---

unofficial information center for the zoo, and the chickens could be counted on to have the latest gossip.

"Have you heard about the visitors coming next week?" one chicken asked a payroll clerk.

"You mean the research team?"

"Don't kid yourself. Everyone's got it figured out. Colonel is being forced out by Zoolandia."

"You're joking. I heard it was just a bunch of researchers. You know—eggheads."

"Hah. You've led a sheltered life kid. What is there to research? I'll tell you, what. They're looking to take it over and they'll get rid of us. Mark my words."

And so the rumor grew, feeding on itself like the ripples from a stone thrown into calm water. By mid-afternoon outraged union representatives had called a meeting of the membership. They would meet that night at the Watering Hole.

Willy Weasel, supervisor of the souvenir shop, heard two of his clerks talking about the union meeting. While he pretended to inspect some merchandise, he listened, then walked back to his office and closed his door. He dialed Charlie Fox, the attorney in Labor Relations.

"Just thought you'd want to know, Charlie. The union is meeting tonight. They might be up to something illegal."

"It's pretty weird for them to call a meeting on such short notice. Got any idea what's up?"

"It's the layoffs."

"What layoffs?"

Willy's voice became conspiratorial. "It's okay. You don't have to let on, Charlie."

Charlie was puzzled. "Thanks for the info, Willy."

"Sure thing. Let me know if there's anything I can do."

Charlie Fox was deceptively mild-mannered. One of the smallest animals at the zoo, he relied on his intellect and sharp wit for survival. This information from Willy was unsettling. How could something this big have developed without his knowing about it? He decided to call the union rep in Stage Productions.

"Julia Peacock," rang out the dramatic voice. Julia was the creative spirit in stage productions, and though she was past middle age, her beauty and flair for the dramatic had hardly diminished

"Julia, it's Charlie." His voice was friendly, conversational.

"Charlie, just the one I want to talk to. What's going on around here anyway?"

"That's what I was wondering." Charlie began, but Julia cut in.

"My crew are beside themselves with worry about this layoff. You might have warned us."

"Believe me, Julia, no layoffs are planned. I would have told you if there were," Charlie assured. "I'm concerned about the union meeting tonight. Any idea what's up?"

"Sure. They're going to talk about the layoffs you say aren't going to happen. Hope you're right, Charlie."

Charlie sat for awhile after he put the phone down. The first thing he needed to do was find his boss, Roy Raccoon, vice president of Personnel and Labor Relations. Charlie could barely conceal his contempt for Roy, who enjoyed Colonel's protection as a "charter member" of the zoo. Roy thought it terribly disloyal for the employees to have voted in a union. After all, hadn't Colonel always taken care of everyone? A handshake was all that was needed, not a union. Roy was consistently uninterested in union activities.

Charlie found Roy in his office, staring out the window. He was offended by Charlie's question and startled by his tone of voice.

"Layoffs? What layoffs? Don't you start this fear-mongering, Fox! If it weren't for those union troublemakers, this kind of rumor would never get started!" As far as Roy was concerned, the subject was closed. Charlie would have to deal with this problem himself.

• • •

The Zoolandia Tiger Team—four tigers and a lioness—arrived the next week. Colonel welcomed them profusely, but he was uncharacteristically nervous. The tigers were polite and impersonal as they swept through the zoo in a practiced way, measuring everything and making endless notations. They spoke to no one. The animals were too intimidated to approach, but they couldn't help noticing how the visitors all looked alike—they were all large cats.

On the last night of the visit, the Tiger Team met in Colonel's boardroom to put together its report. One tiger after another reported out. Nothing had escaped their attention: they discussed the buildings, the equipment, the procedures, and the animals.

As the meeting progressed and the hour got late, Sweeper Bear arrived to clean the administration building. Young and strong, Sweeper was in his prime. As he lumbered along the walk he noticed the light in Colonel's boardroom. "Better turn that light off right away," Sweeper thought. "Colonel don't like wastin' electricity." As he approached the boardroom door, he realized the tigers were meeting inside. He resisted the impulse to run for cover and stood quietly until his heart slowed to a normal beat. He clutched his pail, rags, and Lysol® as he inched his way to the door. He leaned close to hear.

At that moment the Tiger Team was finishing discussion of Jane Porcupine, manager of Purchasing.

"She's rigid and judgmental," Archie Tiger was saying. "I understand she often refuses to place orders on approved purchase orders."

"What does she base her decisions on?"

"Oh, a variety of things, from what I hear. If she doesn't think it's necessary, if she thinks it's too expensive, or if she doesn't like the animal. Those are just some of the reasons I picked up."

"What should we do with her?"

"Promote her, of course." Archie replied.

Everyone laughed, but the irony was lost on Sweeper.

"They're gonna promote that bitch porcupine. I can't believe it," Sweeper shook his head. Suddenly he began to grasp what he was hearing. He'd better write this stuff down. Sweeper headed for Colonel's office to search for a paper and pencil.

Meanwhile the discussion continued.

"We need to get rid of Elephant as soon as possible," said Mike Tiger, the team leader.

"He's like a father," another Tiger added. "As long as he's here, the animals will resist change."

"That's what I was thinking, too." said Mike. "I have an idea. We'll use someone as interim president, not one of the good old boys. I think Luke Shark would fill the bill."

"You're right about one thing. He's not one of the boys. No one likes him."

"He's the perfect choice then, isn't he?" Mike concluded.

Sweeper had hardly stationed himself outside the boardroom again when one of the tigers suggested they take a break. He could hear chairs scraping as the tigers got up from the table as he searched frantically for a hiding place. The safest place was the latrine. He crouched on a toilet seat inside a stall as the tigers entered. Sweeper could barely breathe. The tigers continued.

"What's your assessment of the buildings?"

"They're all outdated. We'll have to raze them."

"Including the outdoor latrines?"

"Yes, they'll be razed, too."

"Well, the sooner the better. When will you have a crew out here?"

"I'm going to use Happy Valley mules and rhinos for that. It's cost-effective and we can start sooner."

Sweeper stepped down and peeked through the space around the stall door. Everyone had gone. He tiptoed to the door, slipped into the hall, and headed for Colonel's office. Then he heard a door open behind him—the Lioness was coming from the females' latrine. He jumped into an open doorway and waited for her to pass. That was enough excitement for him. He gathered his bucket and supplies, put them away, and left the building to head straight for the Watering Hole.

• • •

In a quiet corner of the Watering Hole, Wendy Woodpecker and Jane Porcupine sipped berry juice between spurts of conversation. Their friendship went back many years, to the days when Jane had worked in the souvenir shop.

Wendy was a large bird with a sharp tongue and a big heart. She had been Colonel's executive secretary since Colonel took over as president. They had been like partners. Wendy confided her fear of Colonel's strange behavior.

"I'm beginning to feel paranoid, Jane. He's being so secretive. I keep wondering what I've done. I wish he'd just come out and tell me."

"It's not you. Everyone has noticed how strange he's been."

"Well, if it's not me, what is it?"

"So far it's just a rumor, but there's something up for sure. Those tigers don't look like researchers to me. They look hungry and I hope they don't come back."

"Colonel sure is nervous around them. I've never seen him so ill at ease. That sprinkler business didn't help."

"What sprinkler business?"

"You'll probably hear about it sooner or later, anyway," Wendy said. She looked around to make sure no one could hear, then leaned across the table toward Jane.

"This afternoon, while two tigers were inspecting Hippo Park, the sprinkler system went on. They were dripping wet when they went into Colonel's office. Evidently their camera equipment was ruined," she said in a lowered voice.

"You're kidding! I love it!" Jane choked with laughter. "Who did it? Do you know?"

"No one knows. Colonel was furious. He was ranting about firing the whole maintenance department."

"Did anyone get fired?" Jane leaned close.

"No, you know Colonel would never really fire anyone. He just dictated a memo."

"What did it say?"

"He said he was embarrassed by animals hanging around the fences, looking as if they had nothing to do. Then he said he would investigate the sprinkler incident. He called it inexcusable."

"Is that all?" Jane was disappointed.

"Pretty much. Oh. He said there was no truth to the rumor about an acquisition."

Jane and Wendy didn't notice Sweeper's arrival at the bar. He headed for the tables at the back of the room, where the maintenance workers gathered. Within minutes the monkeys, mules, seals, and rhinos scraped their chairs to Sweeper's table.

"What's going on over there?" Wendy asked, bobbing her head toward Sweeper's table.

"Beats me. Maybe they're doing one of those sports pools."

Sweeper tried to shush everyone.

"They're gonna take over the zoo, that's for sure. That's why they're here. And that's not all. They're gonna lift up all the buildings and the latrines too—raise 'em right up. You mules and rhinos hafta do it, too."

"The hell we do," one of the mules grumbled. "We ain't climbing no scaffolding to build two-story latrines."

"Pipe down. Let him finish. What else did ya hear?"

"Let's see." Sweeper paused to gather his thoughts. "They're gonna promote . . ." Sweeper stopped short and stuck his head above the crowd to survey the rest of the bar. When he saw Jane, he put his head down.

"They're gonna promote a worker that you'd never guess. And you won't like it neither. Don't look now, she's sitting over there. Get this, they're gonna promote that bitch porcupine," he whispered.

All heads at Sweeper's table lifted and turned to look at Jane. All the heads shook and turned back to Sweeper.

Willy Weasel and his wife, Priss, were close enough to hear bits of Sweeper's report.

"Do you think the tigers talked about you, Willy?"

"I don't know." Willy continued to listen and watch, his sharp little eyes darting around the room.

"Why don't you go ask?"

"Not now."

"Well, what are you going to do?" Priss's voice took on a whine. "Now's your chance. Get your foot in the door."

"Okay, okay. Let's get out of here. I have calls to make."

As Willy and Priss walked out, they ran into Jane and Wendy, also heading home.

"I just heard something you might like to know, Jane." Willy's eyes were hooded, and his mouth smiled.

"Oh yeah, what's that?"

"Seems Sweeper overheard those tigers talking in Colonel's boardroom. He says they're taking over the zoo. They plan to promote you."

Jane stopped dead.

"You're kidding! Did they say to what? What else did they say?"

"That's all I know." Willy paused and lowered his voice. "Just remember who you heard it from."

By morning the tigers had quietly departed, and Sweeper's news had spread through the zoo. With each telling the stories grew. Sweeper had never had so much attention. But after a few days, the memory of the tigers and the rumors faded, and life settled back to normal.

Early in February, a news release announced the acquisition of Happy Valley by Zoolandia International, Theme Park Division. The announcement hardly made a ripple at the concession stand. But in the weeks following, the animals could hardly ignore the changes announced in a series of memos issued from Zoolandia headquarters.

Zoolandia International

Memorandum
February 15

To: Zoolandia Employees
Theme Park 46
From: Liz Lioness
Dept: Animal Resources
Subject: Memorabilia Replacement

Zoolandia International is happy to welcome the Happy Valley Zoo to its family of theme parks. Membership in the Zoolandia family brings many privileges, among them the opportunity to share the good will engendered by the name Zoolandia International. Customers expect quality and a good time when they see the Zoolandia "Z," and they expect Zoolandia sizzle.

To keep the Zoolandia sizzle image before the public, we must insist that only products with the Zoolandia logo be used. All employees are to bring any memorabilia with the Happy Valley logo to the souvenir shop for exchange. The shop will carry a full line of Zoolandia items and provide reasonable exchange for any Happy Valley merchandise.

We appreciate your prompt attention to this matter.

Zoolandia International

Memorandum
February 20

To: Happy Valley/Zoolandia Staff
From: Elliott Elephant
 President
Dept: Theme Park Division
 Zoolandia International
Subject: The Zoolandia Way

Welcome to the Zoolandia family of theme parks. I am delighted that Zoolandia will be enriched by your wealth of experience.

Like any family, we have goals. Number One is to entertain our customers. We want them to leave Zoolandia theme parks planning a return trip. How can we assure this? With Zoolandia sizzle. "Sizzle" means a spanking clean facility, state-of-the-art amusement rides, impeccably groomed, _aggressively_ natural animals, and smiling employees. "Sizzle" means turning up the volume, cute is extra cuddly, and scary is positively terrifying. "Sizzle" means return customers and increased revenue--the first step to profit.

Cost control is Zoolandia's second step to profit. We deliver "sizzle" at minimum cost. This keeps us competitive.

Like any family, we have rules: a set of policies and procedures we know to be effective. We call them "the Zoolandia Way." You will find these rules to be in the best interests of your facility. You will be hearing more about the Zoolandia Way in the near future.

Once again, welcome to the Zoolandia family.

2

The "Zoolandia Way" officially arrived with indoctrination training for employees. A local, Sheldon Seal was certified by Zoolandia as a trainer, and the workers began a procession through his classroom.

One morning as he was heading for the classroom, a group of maintenance monkeys followed him one after another, mimicking his waddle and chanting, "Sizzling Sheldon and the Zoolandia shuffle." Sheldon knew he was the target of the animals' resentment about the training.

In his classroom, clutter from the day before was left untouched. This happened more and more often. Sheldon sighed as he straightened chairs, picked up trash, cleaned the boards, and prepared for the day. When the rows of chairs filled, Sheldon began.

"Good morning. Today I have the pleasure of introducing you to Zoolandia Corporation. The theme of today's session is 'Living the Zoolandia Way—Implementation Techniques of Sizzle.'"

Sheldon launched into the familiar routine. But he felt sad at the sullen, resentful stares of the audience.

"These animals were all my friends. Now they look at me as if I'm the enemy," Sheldon thought as he lifted the corners of his mouth and continued his delivery. "Zoolandia Corporation is a worldwide conglomerate made up of eight divisions. This corporation has a proud heritage . . ."

• • •

Meanwhile Ben Bear, vice president of Maintenance, had just arrived at his office. He was late as usual, a privilege earned through long years of service. Ben was small for a bear, and he seemed to shrink as he got older. He was old enough now to retire, but the zoo was his life. He couldn't imagine not coming to his office every day. He and Colonel had practically built the zoo into what it was today, and no one could be prouder of it than Ben. He knew every inch.

Ben looked through the papers on his desk, then threw them back into his IN basket. More queries from those cats at Zoolandia.

"If they're so smart, let 'em figure it out themselves," he grumbled, reaching for his coffee mug. He was concerned about all the questions from headquarters, and for the first time in his career he was worried.

"Morning, Ben," said Joe Rhino, the snakehouse maintenance worker.

Ben grunted in his direction. Morning wasn't Ben's best time.

"I gotta coupla questions from corp this morning. They asked about the snakehouse heating system. Wanted to know the daily temperature readings. Don't that take the cake? Daily temperature readings, what a dang fool idea!" Joe was ready to laugh, but Ben cut him off.

"Don't you worry about it. I'll take care of it."

"What're you gonna tell 'em?"

"Never mind! I said I'd handle it," Ben glared

"Sure, sure Ben. Whatever you say."

The worker left as fast as his lumbering gait allowed. He was well past Ben's hearing when he muttered, "Grouchy old sonuvabitch."

Ben was in a rage. He was a charter member of the zoo, knew it inside and out, and had never been challenged by anyone—ever! He wasn't about to put up with those nosy corp cats snooping around behind his back. He snatched up a piece of paper and scrawled a memo:

"Effective immediately, there will be no direct communication from MY department with Zoolandia personnel. All such communications will be handled personally by ME."

He signed his name to the handwritten memo, nailed it up on the Maintenance bulletin board, and stomped away.

• • •

Roy Raccoon was having a bad day, too. His conversation with Colonel had been disquieting. Colonel was being secretive about his plans.

"If Colonel leaves, I don't know how I'll manage," Roy thought. "Those tigers are cold and heartless. They ask questions I can't answer. I'm exhausted just trying to keep them satisfied. Fox is trying to impress them, and I've no idea what he's telling them."

Though Roy was as fastidious as ever (some said he had a fetish about his appearance), his head was bent low and he walked with a slow stiffness. In his heyday he'd been a powerful figure, and he was hurt when Colonel moved him from operations to personnel. But Roy was nosy by nature and he'd come to appreciate his access to confidential information. He parcelled it out in bits and pieces to keep the animals eager to talk to him. But even that had changed recently, and now the animals hardly noticed him.

Roy was startled at hearing his name called in a loud and insistent voice. Fox was standing in the doorway.

"You don't have to yell, Charlie. You scared me half to death," Roy complained.

"I called you several times, and you didn't hear me. What's so interesting out there anyway? You've been staring out the window for days." Charlie didn't hide his impatience.

No sense telling Charlie he had been thinking about the good old days. Charlie was young, still looking forward, and he wouldn't understand. Roy sighed and began to talk quietly.

"I wasn't looking at anything. I was thinking about how things are changing. It used to be that we could count on Colonel to look out for us. If he said he'd do something, that's all we needed to know. "

Roy was lost in spite of himself in talking about the past. He'd completely forgotten Charlie, who left the room as he rambled. Just last week, when Roy had called in sick, he'd rambled too. He told Charlie he didn't have to put up with all of this Zoolandia nonsense. He could retire any time he wanted, and maybe he would. He'd go live with his daughter. She'd been pressing him and his doctor had been warning him about his blood pressure again. Yes sir, he just might retire. After all his years of Happy Valley service, he didn't have to tolerate this commotion! Charlie felt a brief twinge of sympathy for Roy.

Charlie wiped his brow. He was sweating and his paws were shaking. He'd been working long hours, rarely taking time for meals. It wasn't safe to be away from the office—things were happening too fast. With Roy completely out of touch, it was more important than ever for Charlie to be sharp.

Charlie headed down the hall to the vending room, popping two antacid tablets and a pain pill into his mouth. He poured himself a cup of coffee and pumped money into one of the vending machines. This was his second pack of cigarettes today and it wasn't yet noon. He realized he hadn't eaten since lunch time the day before. He dropped some change into another machine and selected "Sugar Treats."

Millie Pigeon, supervisor of Benefits, came into the vending room just as Charlie was leaving.

"Hi, Charlie. I'd ask how you're doing, but it's obvious just by looking at you."

Charlie frowned, but Millie continued. "You've been working long hours, Charlie. Plus all that coffee and those cigarettes are beginning to show. You look terrible. Absenteeism is skyrocketing, Charlie, and at the rate you're going, you'll be a statistic yourself."

Charlie interrupted.

"What's that about absenteeism?"

"I'm going to talk to Roy about the numbers today. They're pretty alarming."

"Don't bother Roy, Millie. I'm the one who's responsible. How about coming to my office at three? We'll review the numbers and put together a game plan."

"Okay, Charlie. If you're sure I should talk to you. See you at three. AND I'm going to ask if you ate lunch!"

Charlie headed back to his office. He liked Millie, but her nagging was irritating. As he settled into his chair, the phone rang.

"Fox here," Charlie answered

Sheldon Seal sounded upset.

"What's up, Sheldon? I'm pretty busy."

"So am I. I'm just on a break from the sizzle session. I'll make this quick. You've got to do something about Sweeper and his cleaning crew. My classroom's a mess every morning, dirtier than when I left it the night before. I'm under enough pressure with this training. I'm about at the end of my rope. Animals make fun of me. They think I don't hear them, but I do. They used to be my friends. What're you going to do about this mess, Charlie?" Sheldon was just warming up.

"Sheldon, Sheldon, calm down. I can't get a word in edgewise. I know you're upset. I don't blame you. You're in a tough spot. I'll do what I can." Charlie paused. "And Sheldon, you still have friends."

Charlie hung up, wondering whether the chaos would ever end. The phone jarred him back: Liz Lioness from Zoolandia.

Charlie's voice was warm and cordial.

"It's great to hear from you. I've been putting together a report on the union contracts including dates and terms. I'll be ready to give you a full briefing . . ."

"I'm not calling about that." Liz interrupted. "I just had a disturbing piece of news."

"What's that?"

"I understand Ben Bear told his workers not to talk to corporate headquarters. That is intolerable. I'd like you to check on it and call me back immediately." The phone clicked dead.

As Charlie started for Ben's office, his phone rang again.

"Let the damned thing ring," he muttered.

Two hours later Charlie had to tell Liz that her information about Ben was correct. And Ben refused to change it. Charlie's paws were shaking as he talked to Liz. He could feel the acid in his stomach. He grabbed another cigarette, then noticed one was already burning in the ashtray.

Millie stood in the doorway. It was already three o'clock, and one look told her Charlie was in no mood to talk about his eating and working habits. She launched into her report.

Charlie was having a hard time concentrating. Too much was happening at once. Suddenly he realized Millie had stopped talking. She looked at him quizzically.

"Well, Charlie, should I send out the memo about absenteeism or not?"

"Sure, sure, Millie. Whatever you think." Charlie didn't want to admit he hadn't heard Millie's question. He was tired and wanted to finish the meeting. He still had to talk with Sweeper about Sheldon's classroom before he could go home. It was already a long day.

• • •

The next morning Colonel sat in his office, watching the activity outside his window. He had very little to do. Everything was being run from headquarters. The ringing phone startled him. Except for the occasional call from his wife or Roy, his phone hadn't rung in weeks.

"Good morning. Ewald Elephant here," he answered with his old flourish.

"Good morning, Ewald. It's Elliott. How's it going?"

"Well, I'm a bit bored to tell you the truth, Elliott. How much longer do you expect me to stay?"

"That's why I'm calling, Ewald. We've been able to arrange for you to leave at the end of this week."

"My, that's very sudden, Elliott. Not much time to plan my farewell party—only four days." Colonel thought out loud. "Oh well, it doesn't have to be all that fancy, just a simple dinner with champagne, a few speakers . . ."

"I'm afraid you're going to have to scratch the farewell party, Ewald," Elliott broke in

"Why on earth would I do that?" Ewald was stunned.

"Now don't get excited, Ewald. I think it would be best for the animals if you left quietly. Remember, we're trying to ease into the changes, and your party would remind them that things are different. I'm sure you don't want to upset your animals unnecessarily."

Colonel was trapped. He wanted his farewell party, but he would seem selfish if he insisted.

"I'm more disappointed than I can tell you. But if you think it's absolutely necessary, I'll do it."

Colonel leaned back in his chair too hurt to move. He felt as if he were sneaking out, leaving his family behind without farewell.

• • •

On the other side of the administration building, Luke Shark prowled through his finance department to see who was and wasn't at work. He enjoyed the fear he generated and the undertow of whispers rustling ahead. He never let anyone forget who was in charge.

In two years at Zoolandia, Luke had not made a single friend. He lived alone and he never talked about personal matters at the zoo. The rumor was that he had a sinister past, possibly as a "terminator" for a mobster. Though never confirmed, the rumor made animals wary of Luke.

The phone was ringing when Luke reached his office.

"Shark here."

"It's Mike Tiger."

Luke became keenly alert. Mike was head of the Tiger Team. "Good morning, Mike." Luke's voice was smooth. "How are you?"

"Fine, fine. Say Luke, I have urgent business I want to go over with you. Hop on the afternoon flight and be in my office first thing tomorrow."

Luke's pulse raced. Was this good or bad news?

"Sure, Mike. Should I bring anything along?" Luke's voice trailed off.

"No, I have everything I need right here. See you tomorrow."

Luke sat quietly, a long time, so still he looked asleep. His mind was working—fast. He listed possible scenarios and designed strategies for each. Then he grabbed the latest balance sheet and began pouring over it. Dismal. He'd been pressuring Hog to massage the numbers but the ensuing versions didn't look better.

"I'd better get Hog to make one more edit today. I'll take it with me just in case," Luke thought as he headed out of his office.

Luke rarely made phone calls. He preferred to startle his workers by showing up at their desks. Hamilton Hog, the controller, was sitting with his Ben Franklin eyeglasses halfway down his snout, adding rows of numbers. Hog used the glasses as a prop. When he wasn't looking at numbers, he pushed them up on his forehead. His workers used the position of his glasses as a barometer. Never approach Old Man Hog when his glasses were down. Luke had no such qualms. He strode into Hog's office.

"I thought I told you to fix these numbers." Shark's voice was icy. Intimidated, Hog replied, "I did."

"Well, you didn't get it right, Hog. I'm going to headquarters tomorrow and I want a decent balance sheet. Get one ready immediately! Is that clear?"

"What do you expect me to do in a few hours? Perform miracles?" Hog's panic over rode his caution.

"If that's what it requires, do it."

Hog's workers heard, and for once they felt sorry for Hog. Still, they could hardly wait for Luke to leave so they could pass the word that Luke was going to headquarters.

• • •

Charlie Fox had barely arrived when Sheldon Seal stormed into his office. He ranted so, Charlie could hardly make out what he was saying.

"Sheldon, I can see you're upset, but if you don't slow down I'll never figure out what's happened." Charlie pulled out a chair and motioned Sheldon to sit down. Too agitated to sit, Sheldon kept pacing and wringing his flippers, trying to put his thoughts together.

"I thought you said you'd take care of my classroom problem," Sheldon began.

"I talked to Sweeper last night, and he assured me your classroom would get special attention," said Charlie.

"Special attention!" Sheldon shrieked. "It certainly got special attention! You should see it! There's dung smeared on the walls, the chairs've been spray-painted, and there's a stuffed animal on the podium with a dunce hat. It's called 'Mr. Sizzle.' I had to cancel class today. It'll take days to clean the mess up." Sheldon was pacing again.

"What am I going to tell Liz Lioness? She'll find out training's cancelled and it'll be my head."

Charlie was stunned. Feelings ran stronger about sizzle training than he'd imagined. Sheldon was right: Cancelling training wasn't an option. They'd need an alternative site—fast. His mind raced. Then he had an idea, a long shot but worth a try. The Happy Holiday Hotel had meeting rooms and just might be willing to help out. After all, the hotel was hoping for increased business from Zoolandia. Charlie picked up the phone and dialed the hotel. Ten minutes later the problem was solved.

Sheldon was overcome with relief and gratitude. He looked at Charlie with renewed respect.

"How can I thank you, Charlie? If we pull this off, it'll be nothing short of a miracle."

"No problem, Sheldon." Charlie acted casual, but he was just as excited as Sheldon. "We'd better go see Ben. He's gonna have to do quick work on that classroom. We'll have him beef up security, too."

Two hours later Sheldon was back, as panicked as before. He had started calling animals before he realized they had no way to get to the hotel, he explained as he paced.

"Oh dear, oh dear," he said

"Look, Sheldon, it's your turn to use some imagination," said Charlie. "There must be a way to get them there."

"I've got it!" Sheldon exploded. "I'll use one of the trams. The tours don't start until ten and the last one's at four. That'll work perfectly." Sheldon was off like a flash for the tram station.

"When will this end?" Charlie sank into his chair and put his head in his paws. He looked at the overflowing ashtray. His coat was dull, and his headaches were getting worse. And here came Roy Raccoon in a rush. His face was flushed and his pupils were dilated.

"It's the worst, I tell you." Roy cried, facing Charlie.

"What are you talking about, Roy?" Charlie was afraid Roy would have another of his spells. "Sit down and relax."

"It's the worst, I tell you."

"Roy, calm down. Now tell me, what's the worst?"

"Colonel's leaving Friday. Just like that! They told him to pack up and get out. It's just the worst. I don't know, I don't know." Roy was shaking his head back and forth.

Charlie was shocked, too.

"Roy, think a minute, and calm down . . . Now tell me everything you know and go very slowly so you don't miss a thing." Charlie felt as if he were talking to a child.

"I just talked to Colonel. Oh dear, this is the worst. I just don't know what I'm going to do. It's the worst."

Charlie waited. No point in trying to calm down Roy.

"He's leaving on Friday. They said no farewell party or anything. Just pack up and leave. I feel sick. I'm going home. This is the worst." With that Roy got up, walked unsteadily out of the room, and headed for the front door.

• • •

The zoo commons was the scene of a commotion the next morning. Sam Penguin, lead tram conductor, had guided the tram to the commons. Sheldon was urging the animals onto the tram for the ride to the hotel for sizzle training. Hilarity reigned. Some animals demanded popcorn for the ride. Sheldon could hardly get them to sit down. They were waving and hooting at the crowd that had gathered to watch. The tram was not intended to hold a department of bears and rhinos, and the wheels looked dangerously flat.

The tram started amid shouts of farewell, a comical sight the animals wouldn't soon forget. Two bears hung off the back roof shouting at the crowd. When the tram was out of sight, the bears jumped down and raced for the woods. They'd rest there until the tram returned. None of that sizzle bullshit for them.

• • •

Luke Shark, newly appointed acting president of Happy Valley Zoo, strode through the accounting department Thursday morning as usual. But he walked with a new swagger, his steely eyes surveying the room. He could see fear and curiosity on the workers' faces.

"They're wondering what happened at headquarters," he thought. His lips barely covered his sharp teeth as he smiled tightly.

"Well, they'll soon find out." Luke strode right past his office towards Colonel's.

Colonel was finishing up his packing. He moved slower and slower, and now he realized he'd been sitting at his desk for an hour, remembering the events of the past two months. He looked up to see Luke walk past Wendy without acknowledgment and into his office.

"You about through in here, Colonel? I've got things to do."

"What do you have to do in here, Luke?" Colonel's trunk curled in anger.

"Maybe you haven't heard. I just got back from Zoolandia headquarters, and I've been named acting president of this zoo."

Colonel stared. Then, before he could regain his composure, Luke continued.

"Come on, Colonel, pick up the pace. I have things to do that won't wait."

"Can't you use your own office while I finish packing?"

"This IS my office." Luke dropped a packet of papers on the desk, grabbed the top one, and strode out to Wendy's desk.

"Have this distributed immediately. I want every animal to have a copy before the end of the day."

Wendy was going to ask him who he thought he was ordering her around like that, but before she opened her beak, Luke continued.

"This is the announcement naming me as acting president of this zoo."

Wendy stared, too, speechless.

"Did you hear me?" Luke demanded.

"Yes, yes," Wendy faltered. "I heard. I'll get right on it."

Colonel shoved the last of his possessions into a box. Clinging to his last shred of dignity, he announced he'd arrange for the mules to pick up the boxes.

Luke hardly acknowledged Colonel as he sat down at the desk and grabbed the phone. First he called Roy Raccoon. Luke ordered Roy directly to his office, and he paused for just a second before saying which office that was. Luke enjoyed hearing Roy's gasp. The cronies who had frozen him out were going to pay. Once he was permanent, he'd get rid of them all.

Roy arrived in record time. Luke could almost smell the fear. The circles around Roy's eyes were deep, and his fur looked grayer than before. Luke looked at him with disgust. Why hadn't Colonel got rid of him years ago?

"I have an assignment for you Roy," Luke said brusquely as he grabbed a packet off his desk.

"Seems Ben's been causing trouble by refusing to let his workers talk to headquarters. Know what they called him? An obstructionist! Yup. They can't have that. There are too many important things to be done here."

Roy was terrified.

"That's too bad, Luke. Maybe I could talk to Ben. Get him to be more cooperative," he whispered.

"You're gonna to talk to him all right, Roy. But it's too late for cooperation. Much too late. As vice president of personnel, you must notify Ben he is being retired from the corporation."

Roy collapsed into a chair and sobbed. Luke was horrified.

"Stop that sniveling. Pull yourself together. Ben has to be notified by noon today. I have other things to take care of once Ben's gone." Luke dropped the retirement packet in front of Roy.

"Be sure to go over this with him so he knows what he's getting. Then stay with him while he cleans out his desk. He's to be off the property by noon."

Luke stepped past Roy and went out the door. Roy could hear Luke telling Wendy to get someone to come help Roy out of his office. He was aware of being lifted to his feet.

"I'll be all right," he stammered. "Please, just leave me be. I'll be all right." He walked towards the door on legs that barely held. His mind was spinning. He couldn't hold on to a thought and he began to talk to himself. Animals stopped and watched as he walked by. He was in agony.

Roy headed for Ben's office. Ben was hunched over his desk in the posture his subordinates recognized as "not to be bothered." Roy walked through the door and leaned against the wall. When Ben saw it was Roy, his irritation disappeared. Roy looked so stricken that Ben jumped up and helped him to a chair.

"What on earth has happened, Roy? You look like death."

"It is death, Ben. It's the death of this zoo and all the things it's stood for all these years. Colonel's gone. Threw him out just like that. Luke is the new president. You know how ruthless he is. It's horrible. He called me—no ordered me—into his office. I've never seen such a monster. You should have seen him, Ben. It was terrible. I'm scared, Ben. I can't take this stress and aggravation."

"We've had some very happy years here, Roy, and we've done some great work, too. Animals like Luke don't last long. He has enemies. No one will give him a hand when he needs it. Luke may be president, but he can't do it without you and me, Roy."

That reminded Roy why he was there. "Ben, you're wrong, you're wrong. It's not going to be that way at all. Luke doesn't need us. He's going to get rid of us and all of Colonel's supporters."

"Roy, you're getting too excited. We've survived worse."

"Ben, listen to me. You're being forced to retire. No, no—don't say anything, just let me finish. Luke handed me this packet and told me to tell you you're through. He wouldn't even do it himself, the coward! No, Ben, you're wrong. They don't want us."

Ben sat there and looked at the packet. He couldn't make himself reach for it. If he didn't touch it, it wouldn't be true. Still, one look at Roy's face told him it was true. Suddenly Ben let out a roar—a horrible cry of anguish—such as he hadn't let loose in years. Roy just sat there and watched his old friend wrestle with reality.

Bear put his head in his paws, then quietly asked Roy to leave. Roy knew he should go over the packet with Ben and get him started packing his things. But for once in his life Roy decided the company could go to hell. He'd give Ben the courtesy of grieving in private. Roy quietly closed the door as he left. The retirement packet was still sitting on Ben's desk, untouched.

Roy went to his office and closed the door. He needed some time to compose himself, and then he'd go home. He'd call his daughter tonight and tell her he was ready to retire, to move in with her. Yes, that's what he'd do. He felt tired.

"I'll just put my head down, and rest for a minute," he thought, "and then I'll go home."

• • •

Early in the afternoon the animals saw Ben Bear come out of his office. He looked possessed. He went directly to Luke's office, walked in, and slammed the door shut. No one knew quite what happened in that office that day. The roar of their shouts was deafening, but no one could make out the words. Then, silence. Ben came out looking broken. He walked slowly to his office, picked up his lunch bucket, and left for home.

Luke was in a rage like he'd never been before. He grabbed the phone and dialed Roy's office.

"Labor relations, Fox speaking."

"Where the hell is Raccoon?" Luke roared into the phone. Charlie was so startled he didn't answer for a moment.

"He didn't answer his phone and his door's closed, so I answered for him."

"That stupid incompetent was supposed to stay with Ben until he got his stuff cleaned out. I just had a nasty bout with Ben, thanks to Roy. You tell Roy to stay where he is, I'm on my way to see him." Luke slammed down the phone.

Charlie bolted for Roy's office and opened the door. Roy was sitting at the table with his head on his paws.

"Great!" thought Charlie. "Just what I need. He's asleep, and Luke will be here in seconds."

Charlie grabbed Roy's shoulder and shook it.

"Wake up, Roy. Luke's coming and he's in a rage. Something about you and Ben . . ." Charlie quit talking. Something was wrong. Roy wasn't moving. Charlie snatched up the phone and dialed Nurse Goat. Before she could say a word he roared into the phone.

"Get over to Roy's office! I think he's had a heart attack!"

Luke and Nurse Goat arrived at the same time. Luke was shouting about Roy being incompetent. Nurse ignored Luke as she stepped around him and began to check Roy. She looked up and it was clear from the pain in her eyes that there was no need to rush. Roy was dead.

• • •

Pay day was on Thursday, and all the animals looked forward to hoisting a few at the Watering Hole after work. But when word about Roy went through the zoo, no one felt like partying. A note was tacked up on the Watering Hole door: "Closed in memory of Roy Raccoon." Hilarity on the tram returning from sizzle training trailed off as the animals heard the news.

Willy Weasel had had a busy day. He had spent the morning in the storeroom doing inventory, and the news about Luke had come late. Once he heard, he knew big things were happening. Then came the news about Ben and Roy. Willy went into action, and after getting all the facts, he headed for his office and locked the door behind him.

"Mike Tiger will be interested in a lot of things that are going on around here." He picked up the phone.

The memorial service for Roy on Sunday was packed, and everyone had a favorite Roy story to tell. There was not a dry eye in the hall. The last of the charter members was gone. An era was over.

• • •

First thing Monday morning, Luke's phone rang.

"Luke Shark, president, speaking."

"Don't take that title too seriously, Luke. It's just 'acting' president, you know." It was Mike Tiger.

"Oh, hi, Mike." Luke covered his nervousness with humor. "I was just trying it out to see how it sounds."

He paused.

"Actually it has a nice ring to it, so I'll be working real hard to make it a permanent arrangement."

"Well, Mike, what can I do for you?" Luke asked after another silence.

"I've had some upsetting reports about the events on Thursday. I wondered why you hadn't called me about them."

Luke was thinking fast.

"Oh, yes. It was an upsetting day with Roy dying right in his office. Sure felt sorry for the old guy. He was nice enough although he hardly contributed to the zoo in the past few years. I was going to give you a call. It's all taken care of now though."

"Did you talk to the family about the survivors' benefits?" Mike inquired.

"No. I thought I'd get Charlie on that right away this morning."

"Perhaps you aren't aware, Luke," Mike's voice was cold. "Zoolandia has a policy that the family is visited the day the employee dies unless extenuating circumstances prohibit it."

"I'm sorry, Mike. I just didn't think it was that urgent."

"Have you read through that procedure book I gave you on Wednesday?"

"Well, not entirely. But it's been so crazy here . . . "

"So I hear. How did your meeting with Ben Bear go?" Mike was leading up to something.

"Well, actually, I had Roy talk to him. Roy was the expert on personnel and benefits. I thought he could explain it better than I. Besides, I thought Ben would rather hear it from Roy than from me." A long silence followed. Luke began to sweat.

"Zoolandia makes some hard business decisions, Luke, but we don't condone or tolerate cruelty."

Luke's heart skipped a beat.

"Are you telling me you think I've been cruel?" Luke tried to sound surprised.

"Yes."

Silence.

"Tell me, Luke. Who went over the retirement package with Roy before he saw Ben?"

"No one did. I thought he'd understand it. After all, he was supposed to be an expert in those matters."

"Did it ever occur to you that Roy knew nothing about Zoolandia retirement policy?" Mike's voice was icy.

"You're right, I messed up. I just had too much on my mind at once."

"Who is going to do the follow up call on Ben Bear, Luke?"

"Charlie can do it. I don't think it should be me. Ben and I didn't have a cordial parting."

"So I hear."

Luke was thinking quickly. What else did Mike know, and where was he getting his information? There was a serious leak somewhere, and it could be fatal.

"Listen, Mike. This was just a series of circumstances beyond my control. I have a handle on everything now. Take my word for it." Luke tried to sound confident.

"What about the damage to the zoo training room? What's being done about that?"

Luke was stopped dead. What was Mike talking about? He hadn't heard anything about the training room.

"You have heard about it haven't you, Luke?"

"Well, actually just a broad overview. I'm still waiting for the details. Don't worry, I'll handle it."

"One last thing, Luke. Zoolandia considers itself a fair and responsible employer. As acting president, you had better start acting the part. I don't want to hear any more reports of cruelty. Got it?"

"Loud and clear."

"Good."

The phone went dead.

Luke put back the receiver and closed the office door. He needed time to think. He'd have to be careful, at least until he nailed Mike's informant. He didn't want any more unpleasant conversations with Mike.

Just then his phone rang.

"What is it?"

"Luke, it's Radar here." Luke frowned. Radar Dolphin, director of Marketing, was the only zoo animal Luke couldn't intimidate.

"I'm busy Radar. What do ya want?"

"Not much. Just wanted to let you know I'll be going to headquarters for a few months. Indoctrination into the Zoolandia marketing program."

"Fine, fine," Luke said with surprising feeling. He'd be glad to have Radar gone.

"Stay as long as necessary. We'll do fine without you."

Radar chuckled.

"Thanks for the compliment, Luke. And by the way, congratulations on your new position. Expect you and I will be working pretty closely when I get back."

"Not if I can help it," Luke thought as he hung up.

Luke had sent for Duane Beaver, the manager of new construction. Duane was a handsome beaver with thick brown fur, always carefully groomed. When he smiled, which wasn't often, his large white teeth sparkled. When he arrived, Luke greeted him profusely.

"Come in, come in," Luke said as he pulled up a chair. "I've been doing a lot of thinking lately about what a fine job you've been doing. Now that Ben's agreed to retire, I've decided to appoint you acting director of Maintenance."

Duane jumped up from the chair and grabbed Luke's fin.

"Thank you, sir! You'll never regret it. I've just been waiting for the chance to use some of my ideas."

Luke smiled at Duane's obvious enthusiasm. "Now don't get too excited, Duane. I have specific projects for you to start with." Luke handed him a packet.

"Go over this material I've put together and let me know if you have any questions."

"Sure thing, Luke. Thanks again."

Duane rushed off to his office, his large flat tail slapping the ground in excitement.

• • •

Charlie Fox was about to call Liz Lioness when Nurse Goat walked into his office. Nurse was a dedicated manager who had developed a state-of-the-art alcohol treatment program and an innovative nursery for baby animals.

"Luke sent me to talk to you about a problem I'm having. He said he's decided to let you take over Roy's responsibilities while he decides on a permanent solution," she smiled. "Congratulations, I think."

Charlie was surprised.

"Thanks, Nurse. I'd be lying if I said I didn't want the job. I'm surprised Luke has the authority to decide."

"Don't believe everything you hear, Charlie. Luke may just be carrying out what headquarters told him to. He's slippery."

"I'm surprised at you, a sweet thing like you being so suspicious," Charlie teased.

"I'll sweet-thing you, Mr. Fox." She laughed in spite of herself. Nurse took her duties very seriously and brooked no nonsense when it came to the things that mattered to her. Her nursery was one of the best in the industry, and many large zoos came to learn from her.

"I did come here for a purpose, Charlie." Nurse was all business.

"Millie Pigeon has sent out a memo about absenteeism. You know, one of her garbled messages that can be interpreted five ways from Sunday?"

Charlie shook his head. He was all too familiar with her memos.

"Have you seen it, Charlie?"

"No. Unfortunately, I haven't. She did mention it to me though. There was so much going on, I didn't think to check it. I know she wanted to do something about the dramatic increase in absenteeism."

"She did something about it, all right."

Nurse looked at the paper she was holding.

"Listen to this: 'Effective upon receipt of this memo, all employees reporting back to work after any missed time must report to Nurse Goat in the medical office before reporting to their work stations. Ms. Goat will determine whether the absence was due to a legitimate illness and so note on the referenced absenteeism form, which is to be presented to the appropriate supervisor upon return to work.'"

Nurse stopped reading and looked up in exasperation.

"Care to interpret that, Charlie? From what I can tell, anyone who is away from work comes to see me, even if they went to the blacksmith for a broken shoe." Nurse's voice rose.

"This morning I had a line of animals all the way out the door. Charlie, you know as well as I, the absenteeism is a result of this acquisition. What am I supposed to do, turn the animals in for malingering? I can't do that. I won't do that!"

"Don't let it get to you. It'll blow over before long."

Nurse was out of her chair, fast as a wink and mad as a hornet. "Of all the stupid ideas, Charlie, this takes the cake, suggesting I use my time to sign absenteeism forms! Do you have any idea how much I'd like to butt you in the head? You insensitive jerk!" Nurse had a reputation for her temper.

"Nurse, I'm sorry. I really am. It was a thoughtless remark. I just meant it's really crazy now, and we're all doing things we wouldn't normally do."

"Okay, okay. I believe you. But I'm not going to go along with this nonsense Millie has started. These are my friends, and I don't blame them for acting out their frustration. Some days I feel like playing hooky myself, and just who would sign my form?"

"You'd better have Millie retract her memo because I'm signing everything that comes through. You won't catch any fish in my net," Charlie told her.

Charlie was irritated at himself. How many times would he have to undo one of Millie's memos before he began paying attention? He made a note to call her but he first put in a call to Liz Lioness to get a briefing on Ben's retirement package. Charlie intended to be a corporate labor relations attorney someday, and Liz was his best connection for making it happen at Zoolandia.

"Now is as good a time as any to bring up the subject," he decided to himself.

"Liz, I have a question I hope you can answer. Luke has me doing Roy's work, and it looks like he might decide to give it to me permanently. Do you think there'd be any opposition from headquarters? I mean, Roy's job would be a good stepping stone to a corporate job someday."

Charlie stopped talking and waited for what seemed an eternity.

"It's within Luke's prerogative to give you work assignments. As far as a replacement for Roy, you might as well hear it from me. There won't be one. Roy's workers will report directly to headquarters," Liz finally said.

Charlie could hardly believe his ears.

"I never dreamed it would go this way," he said.

"I understand your disappointment, Charlie. I'm aware you've been working hard. I didn't say never. I just said not this time. I'm sorry, Charlie. I really am."

Charlie sat a long time. His hopes were dashed. Rid of an incompetent boss, he now had a bureaucracy. He reached for another cigarette, from his third pack of the day.

3

Charlie Fox was going home for dinner for the first time in weeks. He was cleaning up his desk when the phone rang.

"Fox here."

"Charlie, it's Julia Peacock. Do you have a minute?"

"Sure. I was about to leave, but I always have time for you."

"I'll make it quick, Charlie. I think you'd better have a meeting with the union reps. With all that's happening, we'd better keep in touch."

"I couldn't agree more. Something I'd like to have explained is who messed up Sheldon's classroom," Charlie said. There was a pause.

"You're missing the point, Charlie. It doesn't matter who. The important thing is that the animals are upset enough to do something like this. You've been running roughshod over our contracts, and we've let some things go. But things have been too much around here, even for me," she said.

"Listen Julia. I don't have the luxury of being philosophical. It's cost us thousands of dollars in repairs, not to mention the expense of transporting animals to an alternate site."

"I don't know who made the mess, Charlie, and I don't condone the behavior. I just think it's important to prevent another incident. This rep meeting can be a first step."

"How about if we meet Friday morning in my office?"

"Friday is fine, Charlie. A neutral meeting place would be better than your office. How about the back room at the Watering Hole? It's always empty during the day."

"Whatever you say, Julia. I'll meet you at the Watering Hole."

"See you Friday morning, Charlie. Let's say around nine."

• • •

The next morning Charlie gathered up his papers and headed for Luke's office. Stopping to chat a minute with Wendy, he noticed her desk was uncharacteristically cluttered.

"Morning, Wendy. Looks like you're keeping busy these days."

Wendy looked up, and Charlie could see circles under her eyes. For the first time, she looked old. Her feathers had lost their luster, and her movements were slow and labored.

"Hello, Charlie. Go right in. Luke is expecting you." She turned back to her typewriter and began pecking.

Luke looked like energy itself at the desk.

"Come on in, Charlie. I've been expecting you."

"Morning, Luke." Charlie knew better than to chat. It was strictly business in Luke's office.

"I've been working on the opening position for the negotiations with the janitors, and I'm ready to give you a briefing."

Luke motioned for Charlie to sit down and leaned back to listen. Charlie started on the items, and Luke let him finish before making any comments.

"Listen, Charlie. You've got to get tough with the unions. We're losing money, and we have to tighten our belts. Let them know who's in charge. I won't tolerate more damage. It's your job to keep a lid on."

"I don't think we need to be so hard-nosed, Luke. The unions have given us some leeway on contractual items during the acquisition. We can get more from the unions if we maintain a spirit of cooperation. I'm meeting with the union reps Friday morning to keep the dialog open."

"Don't give me any of that spirit of cooperation. I want you to tighten the screws." Luke shuffled through his papers. The meeting was over.

Charlie nearly collided with Hog, coming up the hall. Hog's head was down, and he was talking to no one in particular.

"This one had better satisfy him. I've had it with Luke and his budget edits." Hog hadn't noticed Charlie at all.

"Oh. Hi, Charlie." Hog was nervous. Had Charlie overheard him?

"What's up, Hog? You look like you've lost your last friend."

"I'm headed for Luke's office. Got another budget edit to go over with him. You know us financial guys, Charlie. Everything's got to be perfect before we give up." Hog gave a weak laugh.

"You look beat. Better slow down. You're not as young as you used to be."

Hog was frightened by the truth of Charlie's observation. Just last week he had had trouble getting his breath on the stairs. He had grabbed onto the railing and waited several minutes before climbing the rest of the way. By the time he reached his office, he was soaked with sweat and his heart was thumping. His vision was blurring lately, too.

"You should talk, Fox. Look at your paws shake. I see you're smoking again. On your third pack yet today?" Hog's voice had a nervous, high pitch.

"I'm still on my first pack, but I'll probably be up to three by tonight. That's what comes of having so much fun."

Hog grunted, then headed to Luke's office. He hadn't gone far before he was muttering again. Then someone was calling him. He turned to see Sarah Giraffe, his manager of planning.

"Are you going in to see Luke?" she asked as she caught up.

"Yes, he asked for another budget edit. I'm sure he's not going to like this one either." Hog breathed heavily, and beads of sweat appeared on his forehead.

"You could take some pressure off by telling him about the budget automation project. You can take my update with you."

"I don't think Luke's interested. Just do what's necessary to keep Zoolandia off our backs. "

"We need a scanner for data input with all the history we have to get into the system. I thought you could ask Luke to approve it."

"We don't need a scanner. Haven't you been paying attention? We're trying to get the budget down, not up. That stupid automation system is never going to work, so don't buy anything." And he was off down the hall.

Sarah turned around purposefully. She intended to get her scanner. She headed to Jane Porcupine's purchasing office. Jane was at her desk, going through purchase orders.

"Hi, Jane. How are you doing?" Sarah asked as she sat down in the only chair not filled with papers.

"I'm very busy, that's how I'm doing."

"Well, this is business, Jane."

"There's no money for purchases, you know." Jane's authority had been drastically cut.

"I don't need a purchase, Jane. I need to rent a computer scanner for the budget automation project."

"I don't know anything about scanners or automation. That's not my department." She reached into her drawer and pulled out a form. "Just fill this in and have Hog sign it. It goes directly to Accounts Payable."

"I need a second signature. Would you sign for me?"

"Are you kidding? Hog told you no, didn't he? If you want to go around him, you'll have to find some one else to help you."

Jane turned away.

• • •

Duane arrived at the construction site of the new restaurant pit near the old picnic grounds. As he got out of his truck to begin his inspection, he noticed a group of workers sitting around smoking. They were deep in conversation. Duane immediately assumed his management posture.

"Hey you over there! What do you think you're doing? This isn't a break time. Get back to work."

As Duane got closer, he saw it was some of the mules.

"What's the meaning of this unofficial break?" he demanded.

Before anyone could answer, he continued, "If I catch any one of you loitering on the job like this again, you're going to be out on your ears. Is that clear?"

No one answered. Everyone just stood and stared.

"Get going, I said."

Duane's voice carried over the construction site. Work stopped and the animals stood where they were to watch. The sudden silence unnerved Duane.

"Now that you've all stopped working, you might as well hear what I have to say, too. Zoolandia is watching this construction very closely, and I don't want any screw-ups. We have a tight schedule, and I don't want to overrun it. If I have to, I'll be down here every day monitoring your work. That's exactly what I'll do if I catch you on unauthorized breaks. You'll put in an eight-hour day or I'll know the reason why."

Silence.

Satisfied that he had made his point, Duane turned, slapped his flat tail on the ground, and hurried back to his truck.

As soon as Duane drove away the workers decided to tell Muley, the union rep, what had happened. They weren't going to put up with Beaver and his bullying. They'd go by the letter of the contract and slow construction to a near halt. That night at the Watering Hole, the word went out. The mules were having a slow-down.

• • •

Friday morning came much too fast for Charlie. He had worked at a frantic pace getting ready for the union rep meeting. Liz Lioness had insisted on attending, another worry for Charlie.

Charlie tried to hide his nervousness from Liz as they walked to the Watering Hole. "This should be short and sweet, Liz. I've got all the information they need, and once they're aware of the facts, I'm sure we can come to some mutual agreements. As a matter of fact, this may just end up being a pleasant visit."

"That would be nice, Charlie. I hope you're right. Actually, there are quite a few things I'd like to check out while I'm here, so a short and sweet meeting would suit me just fine."

Charlie's ears went up.

"Oh? Anything I can help with?"

"No, not that I'm aware of. I'd like to chat with Sarah Giraffe about the budget automation project. Then there's some confusion about sick leave. And, of course, there's always the possibility something else will surface."

"We've been watching sick leave very closely, Liz. We've clamped down on absenteeism and have animals reporting to Nurse when they return to work."

"Has Nurse identified any abuse?"

"No, not that I've heard."

"Then why keep having her do it if it's not getting results?"

"Oh, I didn't say it wasn't getting results. I think the very act of having to check in with Nurse has stopped some of the abuse."

They arrived at the Watering Hole, a small building with a bar that ran the length of the main room. In the light of day its wooden chairs and plank tables looked drab. Charlie was embarrassed when he noticed Liz looking at notices and graffiti on the walls. Posted prominently on the door was the Zoolandia logo, with expletives.

"This is quite a display, Charlie. It looks like the Watering Hole is a poor choice for a meeting with the union reps."

Charlie was furious. He hadn't been in the Watering Hole for months.

"You're right, Liz. This is absolutely inexcusable."

Charlie pushed open the door, and as he entered the meeting room he saw all the chairs but one taken by the union reps for BUZWA (Brotherhood of United Zoological Workers Amalgamated). Sam Penguin, lead tram conductor, was at the head of the table. Evidently he would be the leader. The reps hadn't expected Liz, and there was a look of hostility when she entered. No one offered to get another chair.

The room was too small for ten animals. The temperature was rising, and the odor was strong. Animals sat in stony silence as Charlie began to speak in a conversational style.

"I'm glad to meet with all of you this morning. We've always worked together, and we need to work together now more than ever."

"Cut the crap, Fox," said Sam Penguin. "We're not here to exchange pleasantries. We're here to talk about how you have been walking all over our contracts. And what is *she* doing here? We don't need any interference from headquarters. This is a private, local matter."

"Wait a minute, Sam." Julia rose to her feet. "We don't need to incite a riot first thing. Let's take it a little slower."

Julia turned to Charlie and Liz.

"Sam's right about the contractual abuses, Charlie. We've tried to cooperate, but that brings more abuse. We've decided to take a stand before you completely negate the contracts we have."

Before Julia could continue, Muley began to shout.

"I'm not here to be polite, Lioness or no Lioness. I've got such a mess on my hands that it's all I can do to get my workers to come to work in the morning. Beaver has been on their backs since he got that job. Yesterday he stopped the whole construction project while he chewed out my move crew. He never bothered to ask them anything, just started yelling and insulting them. They were waiting for his instructions on where to put the exterior bricks and mortar. He runs around ordering things but never takes the time to follow through with instructions. He accused them of loitering. And that's after he's been riding them constantly to work double time. Well, he's pushed them too far! We'll handle Beaver all right. He wants to be a jerk, we'll show him how we handle jerks!"

The room, filled with Muley's anger, was silent. Julia was still standing.

"Well, Charlie, as you can see, tempers are flaring. Duane's is just one example of contract mauling. Another is sending all the animals off the property for training. You know that's against our contract, plus the extra duty that created for the tram animals. Hauling all those animals clear into town created all sorts of extra repairs. Those aren't part of the contract, Charlie."

"I can speak for myself, Julia," said Grinder, the monkey from tram maintenance. "Your bright idea of using the tram for a school bus has caused me no end of problems. I've had to order major replacement parts. Several of the monkeys had to work extra hours. Then you gave me crap about paying overtime. You said, I should be able to get my work done in an eight-hour day. 'Featherbedding,' I think is what you called it."

"Look Grinder, we all have to make adjustments during this time of change. It is a temporary solution for something that was caused by someone destroying company property."

"Speaking of destroying company property, what possessed you to tear down the outdoor toilets?" said Amanda Chicken. "You expect the food production hens to take a fifteen-minute break, and then you tear down the toilets! There's no way we can traipse over to the administration building and back in fifteen minutes. There's only two stalls in there and fifty chickens."

Charlie was struggling to gain control of the meeting.

"Look everyone, I'm convinced. You have some legitimate gripes, and I need to hear them all. But there're some things you need to know, too. Then maybe we can come to some agreements that satisfy us all." He began to hand out packets as he talked.

"I've put together some information to help explain. As you can see, the top page is an overview of our current budget. I hope it's not lost on you that we are running in the red. Zoolandia expects us to get that turned around fairly quickly. Right now they're making significant capital investments in Happy Valley with the understanding we'll be repaying those investments from future profits."

The animals looked through the packets as they listened to Charlie. His confidence rose as he spoke.

"The future of Happy Valley is a bright one. We've got new buildings under construction, and Zoolandia is bringing in a whole new technology with the theme park approach. We'll have a secure future if we can just work through this difficult time, but we may have to make some sacrifices for the short term. I don't think it's too much to ask. We're still in this together, pulling for the same goal . . ."

"Cut the bull, Charlie. I've had some glimpses of that wonderful future. Word has it we're going to be wearing costumes, for pete sake." Julia spoke again.

"Now I'm in theatrical productions, where costumes are a way of life, but it's not fair to expect other animals to cavort around in frilly little outfits for the amusement of the customers."

Liz Lioness spoke for the first time.

"I understand what you're saying, Julia. It's not like you imagine. The costumes are tasteful, not meant to embarrass anyone. Some of you might visit a fully operational theme park to see for yourselves."

"Liz has an excellent idea." Charlie jumped in. "Look over those packets, and then if you have any questions, give me a call. In the meantime, let's think about a visit to a theme park."

A tearing sound could be heard, and Charlie looked over to see Sam Penguin ripping his information packet. Very quickly the noise filled the room.

"That's what we think of your information packet, Charlie. It's going to take more than a glib speech and a few pages of propaganda to satisfy us."

Julia leaned forward.

"If you really want to work with the unions, you'd better be willing to do more than that, Charlie. I'd suggest we meet regularly and begin to sort out this mess. Look around you, Charlie. This is not a happy group. We've worked with you in the past, but now all bets are off. Think about it. What do you want? Meet with us or we'll meet without you. It's your choice."

"I didn't mean to imply I wouldn't meet with you, as a group, any time there's something to talk about. I've always had an open-door policy."

"Are you going to meet with us or not?" Muley demanded.

"Yes, of course. Just name the time and place."

"Right here, same time next month."

"That's fine, but you'll have to clean up all the graffiti. It's just unacceptable!"

"It's our room, Fox. The graffiti stays."

"I'm afraid you're mistaken about that, Mr. Mule," Liz began. "The Watering Hole is company property, and it's against policy to have that type of adornment on the walls. Now I hesitate to antagonize you just as you are coming to an agreement, but I support Charlie. The graffiti has to go."

Liz turned to Charlie.

"I think we've made our point, Charlie. We'll see you all on the twenty-fifth of next month at 9:00 A.M."

Liz and Charlie headed back to the administration building. When they reached Charlie's office, Liz closed the door.

"Now let's go over what was said in the meeting, and plan for the next one. Incidentally, Charlie, the budget information you gave them was terribly outdated. If you're going to give them data, be sure it's accurate."

Several hours had passed when Charlie and Liz emerged from his office.

• • •

The next union rep meeting was more organized. Julia opened the meeting with a prepared talk.

"Charlie and Liz, we've decided to tell you how things look from the union perspective. Let's go back to the initial Zoolandia Tiger Team visit. We were told it was a research group. That was a boldfaced lie. Why couldn't you have told the truth? The zoo was a candidate for acquisition, and you all knew it.

"Then you, or Zoolandia, put through changes without telling or asking us anything. This training is a good example. Sizzle training has become a symbol for things that are being done to us.

"The outdoor toilets are another example. You might think it's amusing, but to Amanda and her chickens it's a serious matter. Working for Rodney Rooster is bad enough. Rodney is on them constantly about taking breaks, and he's pressuring them to speed up the pace. Summer is the busiest time of the year, and no summer help has been hired to handle the overload.

"Management thinks Rodney is just great, his production numbers look good, and he keeps his production chickens quiet. But how many complaints have you had about him harassing the chickens? You must know he pressures the young chicks for dates, implying their jobs are on the line if they say no. I know why you haven't done anything about it. Numbers are more important than production chickens who can easily be replaced.

"It's not that easy, Charlie. We're going to file a complaint if something isn't done. There are agencies that handle that sort of thing.

"Look at what happened to Ben Bear. Sure he was management, but it's pretty clear to us that Zoolandia is a hip-shooting organization. If you're in the way, bang—you're dead. You keep talking about the zoo being in the red. That's always the rhetoric before a layoff. Zoolandia is a rich conglomerate, one that can well afford to modernize this place. They plan to make a profit, and they see this zoo as a high potential for profit. So why can't they invest money in the employees, too? They can afford to take a loss for awhile until the zoo gets on its feet. That's the cost of doing business. But they'll want concessions from us, and we'll still suffer a layoff.

"And look what happened to Nurse's alcoholic treatment program. After all the publicity she's received for an outstanding program, Zoolandia has shelved it. If we can't hold our liquor, they'll throw us out, and replace us with someone who can.

"This is rather a long talk, Charlie, and I've still left out a lot of issues."

Julia stopped speaking, and everyone looked at Charlie.

"Perhaps I can address some of the concerns," Liz began. "There is always secrecy attached to an acquisition because of the tremendous fluctuation of stock prices when acquisitions are mentioned in the press. We couldn't tip our hand until the deal was settled. Unfortunately, that had a negative impact on the employees—also a hazard of business. Zoolandia is proud of its reputation for being animal-oriented, and we've had very little employee discontent. We've tried to be as open and communicative with you as we can.

"One thing that is essential in a corporation as large as Zoolandia is to have consistency—like with the alcohol treatment program. We certainly don't have a philosophy of throwing workers out if it's perceived they have a problem with alcohol. Nurse is welcome to become familiar with the Zoolandia procedure and may be a part of that program any time she wants."

"As for layoffs, I can't promise you one way or the other, at this moment. For the long run there will be even more jobs, but we'll have to go through some cutbacks to get there. Now let's work some of the specific issues that you've raised."

When the meeting adjourned, the union reps were in no hurry to break up.

"Nothing is going to come out of these meetings. You just wait and see," Muley grumbled.

"You're probably right, Muley," Julia agreed, "but we don't have any good alternatives just now. I think we should have our own meetings on a regular basis. If we hang together, we can put more pressure on Zoolandia. How about meeting again in two weeks?"

Everyone agreed to Julia's idea. Tough times were coming, and they were going to need each other.

• • •

On Monday morning Luke was shocked to find Mike Tiger waiting for him in his office.

"This is a pleasant surprise, Mike. Welcome to Happy Valley."

"Morning, Luke. I thought I'd deliver this announcement in person. There aren't any surprises, but you'd better look it over before you send it out."

While Luke read the memo, Mike looked out the window. He could see the restaurant pit construction area, a beehive of activity. He recognized Duane Beaver walking among the workers. Duane was energy itself, waving in all directions as he gave instructions. Something caught Mike's eye. The pit area looked odd.

"It's that hut in the center. We don't have anything like that in the plans. I'd better check it out," he thought as he turned back to Luke.

"There's one more piece of business I'd like to go over with you, Luke. We need to cut back on the number of employees at Happy Valley. I'm sure that's no surprise to you."

Zoolandia International

Memorandum
June 2

To: Zoolandia Employees
Theme Park 46
From: Michael H. Tiger
Corporate Vice President
Dept: Zoolandia Theme Park Division
Zoolandia International
Subject: Organization Announcement

Zoolandia International is pleased to announce the designation of Happy Valley Zoo (Theme Park Number 46) as a stand-alone profit center. This status change necessitates a realignment of the management structure to further focus attention on corporate standardization of practice.

Luke Shark will continue as Acting President. Effective immediately, reporting to Mr. Shark will be:

- Vice President of Operations, Carl Crocodile
- Vice President of Marketing, Radar Dolphin
- Director of Maintenance, Duane Beaver (acting)

Support functions requiring use of corporate-wide systems will report directly to Zoolandia. Reporting to Zoolandia will be:

- Manager of Personnel & Labor Relations, Charles Fox
- Vice President of Finance and Administration, Hamilton Hog (acting)

I solicit the cooperation of every employee in helping these management personnel be successful in their new and revised responsibilities.

"It's not a surprise, Mike. I was just hoping it wouldn't come to a layoff."

"I'm not talking about a layoff yet, Luke. What we're going to do first is offer a voluntary retirement program. This is a fairly mature employee population, so we may be able to make substantial reductions with this offer. The memo is all drawn up and ready to distribute, but I don't want the animals to associate my visit with employee cuts, not even a voluntary one."

"Sure Mike. I'll date it for Wednesday and distribute it then."

"Good. That's all for now, Luke. I thought I'd spend the day walking around and chatting with the workers."

"That's a great idea. I'll come with you."

"No thanks, Luke. I'd rather just go around by myself."

"Okay, Mike, whatever you say. I think you'll find the animals are pretty happy with the way they've been managed here. I've certainly been trying to keep them happy."

"I'll soon see, won't I?"

Luke was worried.

"I don't want him wandering around here on his own. There's no telling what he'll dig up. I'd better keep an eye on him, just in case," he thought.

Luke began to stroll down the hall in the direction Mike had gone. Mike was walking through the administrative area when he heard loud voices coming from one of the offices.

"Look, Jane, you have to do something right away. I'm completely out of popcorn bags, and you know popcorn is my biggest moneymaker," said Rodney Rooster.

"That's not my problem, you know. If you had put your order in soon enough, you wouldn't be having this problem. Don't come in here, and pester me about it."

"I'd say it is your problem, Jane. I put the order in two months ago. There's no excuse for those bags not getting here by now."

"Are you accusing me of not ordering your stupid bags?" Jane demanded.

"Well, have you ordered them?"

"Of course I have, you ignoramus."

"When did the order go in?"

"How should I know? I can't remember every little order I put through."

"Suppose you just reach in your drawer and check?" Rodney's voice was high in pitch, and his comb was quivering.

"I'll have to check and get back to you. Your popcorn bags aren't the most important thing in my life, you know."

Mike walked in as Jane finished.

"Hello there. I heard your voices in the hall. Sounds as if you two could use a mediator."

Jane's mouth began to move, but nothing came out at first.

"Oh no, not at all," she chuckled. "Rodney and I go at each other like this all the time. It's just our way of teasing."

Jane turned to Rodney.

"I'll check into those bags right away, Rodney."

"So you're Rodney Rooster. I've been hearing about you. How about showing me your food production operation?"

"It'd be my pleasure, Mr. Tiger. Yes sir, it'd be my pleasure. " Rodney was practically crowing as he walked out with Mike.

"I hear you've been very effective with keeping productivity up through all of the changes, Rodney. That's a great accomplishment and hasn't gone unnoticed," Mike said. He paused and looked at Rodney, whose head was cocked back proudly.

"However, it's also come to my attention that there's potential for a sexual harassment complaint to be filed against you. If there's any truth to that information, I'd suggest you clean up your act, Rodney. We don't tolerate that sort of thing, ever. It's grounds for on-the-spot termination if it's substantiated."

Rodney looked as if he had been hit by a truck.

"I can assure you, sir, that I have conducted myself with the highest standards. I pride myself on my professionalism, and I would never do anything to give that impression."

"Good, Rodney. I'm glad to hear that. I'd hate to see you mess up a promising career by doing something foolish."

Eventually Mike reached the construction site. Sure enough, there was the hut he had noticed from Luke's office.

"Now who in the world had this brainstorm?" he wondered. He'd tell Duane Beaver to tear it down. One thing Zoolandia didn't tolerate was deviation from plan.

"Hello there," Mike yelled to a couple of construction workers hauling bricks. They put down their wheelbarrows and walked over.

"Hi, Mr. Tiger. Nice to see ya," one mule said respectfully.

"Thanks, I'm glad to be here. There have been a lot of changes since I was here last. Looks like plans are moving along nicely. Are you having any problems?"

There was a pause.

"Maybe we shouldn't be talking about it, but Beaver's been hassling us. He abuses us workers, all the time yelling at us for nothing."

"That doesn't sound good. I'll check it out. Where can I find Duane?"

"On the other side of the construction site. Ya won't have trouble finding him. Ya can hear him a mile off."

Sure enough, Mike heard Duane before he saw him. He was waving and shouting.

"That's just how he looked when I saw him through the window," Mike thought. "Does he do anything besides wave and shout?"

"Mr. Tiger, this is a pleasant surprise. I was hoping you'd stop by to look at the construction site. We're making excellent progress."

"It looks like things are moving along nicely. I'm concerned about the hut I saw in the restaurant pit. Is that some type of temporary structure?" Tiger asked.

"No, no." Duane said. "It was to be a surprise, a touch I've added. I think you'll agree, it's a good idea."

"Duane, it may be a great idea, but you can't deviate from the Zoolandia plans. Every theme park has the identical restaurant pit area."

"I was sure you'd be pleased when you saw it completed. How about if I take you over there and show you?"

"No. Tear that structure down immediately, and in the future if you have an idea, submit your plans to the facilities design group first."

"Yes, sir. I'll have it down immediately. I'm sorry to have caused a problem sir. I wasn't thinking."

"Zoolandia is not like Happy Valley, Duane. It's a large conglomerate with rules and regulations. I commend your enthusiasm. Just don't let it get you into trouble."

"No, sir, I certainly won't."

"One last thing. There seems to be some discontent among your workers. Better keep an eye on it."

"Yes, sir. I'll get them straightened out."

Mike headed back to the administration building. It had been a long day and he was beat. Just before he reached the door, he heard someone calling his name.

"Hello, Mike. You remember me, Willy Weasel?"

"Hello, Willy. Yes, I remember talking to you on the phone some time ago. How are you?" Mike voice was cool and polite.

"Just fine, Mike. Thought I'd catch up with you, and fill you in on what's really been happening around here." Willy was conspiratorial.

"I appreciate the offer, Willy, but I have a flight to catch.. Perhaps the next time I'm in town."

Mike went into the building. Willy was stunned.

"After all the snooping around, and information gathering I've done for that S.O.B., he snubs me. I'll show him. No one snubs Willy Weasel."

When Mike reached Luke's office, Luke was sitting at his desk looking busy. Mike noticed mud on Luke's suit.

"Well, Luke, I've had a nice day. Looks like things are working quite well around here."

"Thanks, Mike. I think so, too. Where all have you been?"

"Just about everywhere. And I've picked up some interesting information here and there."

"Oh?" Luke's voice was casual. "Anything I should know about?"

"I don't think so. You should get out and around yourself, Luke."

"I try, Mike, but most days I'm tied up in my office with a mountain of paperwork."

Zoolandia International

Memorandum
June 4

To: Zoolandia Employees
Theme Park 46
From: Liz Lioness
Dept: Animal Resources
Subject: Zoolandia Greener Pasture Plan

The Zoolandia Greener Pasture Plan (ZGPP) will go into effect beginning next Monday for a period of 30 days. The intent of ZGPP is to provide mature animals an opportunity to retire from active employment at Zoolandia.

Zoolandia has thirty years of experience with ZGPP and many success stories of animals who have built interesting and innovative second careers after taking advantage of ZGPP.

ELIGIBILITY: Animals must have twenty-eight years of employment with the company.

BENEFITS: Eligible animals electing ZGPP within the 30-day pasture period receive:

- Half-pay until normal retirement age is attained, at which time normal retirement benefits begin.
- Retraining not to exceed five full days for new professions outside zoo-keeping.
- Relocation to and one month's lodging at any Zoolandia location at which a retiree intends to settle for retirement or for a second career.
- Continuance of health insurance for self and family for six months at same rate.
- Investment counseling from Zoolandia experts.
- Lifetime passes to any Zoolandia facility.

Details and personal counseling are available in the Personnel and Benefits offices for all eligible employees.

4

The voluntary retirement program announced on Wednesday was the only topic of conversation among the workers that day. Everyone was surprised; eligible workers were downright stunned. The animals had thirty days to make a decision. Zoolandia counselors would begin informational seminars and individual counseling sessions the next week.

On the day of the announcement, Wendy Woodpecker and Jane Porcupine had lunch in the executive conference room, as they often did. It gave them a feeling of exclusiveness not to have to eat in the employee cafeteria.

"I'm so upset, Jane, I just don't know what I'm going to do." Wendy was hardly touching her food. "Luke said I'd better take the retirement plan."

"He can't do that, Wendy. You can file an age discrimination complaint if he tries to force you out." Jane was indignant. "It's the same old story. Use us and throw us aside. Maybe it's time we females started fighting back."

"Jane, it's no use. I don't have any fight left in me. Temporary agencies can always use good secretaries. Maybe I can do that as long as my health is good . . . "

"Well, you may not have much fight left in you, but I have enough for the both of us. I'm not going to take this sitting down."

"Take what sitting down, Jane? They aren't forcing you out too?"

"Well, no. Of course not. But I'm in for a big promotion, and they haven't acted on it. I'm going to demand they put it through immediately," Jane said over her shoulder as she flounced out the door.

Later that day, Willy Weasel visited Jane.

"What brings you over here Willy? I never see you unless it's trouble."

"Actually, Jane, I thought you and I might have some common interests. We could pool our efforts."

"I can't imagine what you're talking about, Willy."

"I'm sure you can't, so I'm going to tell you, Jane. Those Zoolandia cats are going to toss us aside as soon as it's convenient for them. I have some inside information about what happened to Roy Raccoon. Officially, they called it a heart attack."

Willy let that sink in.

"Just what are you getting at, Willy? You're beginning to give me a scare."

"I can't talk about it, but there are some devious things going on. You and I could work together to fight off this takeover. We need to make this place unprofitable enough that Zoolandia will sell it to the employees."

"I don't know, Willy. It sounds like a crazy idea."

"Let me know. If you don't get in on the start, we may not let you in later." Willy softly closed the door.

• • •

When Liz and Charlie arrived at the third union meeting, there were still empty chairs.

"Good morning," Charlie greeted the table at large. "I see we have a couple members missing."

"They'll be late. There are problems at the construction site."

"Let's get started. Should we recap the last meeting?"

"That's not necessary, Charlie. We remember," Sam Penguin said. Sam began a tirade on the difficulties of trying to maintain tram rides when the zoo was a battle zone of construction.

As Sam took a breather, the door burst open and Muley and Arnold walked straight to Charlie and Liz.

"Isn't it convenient you're both here? Now I won't have to say this twice," Muley brayed. "This is the last straw! Beaver just told me he fired two workers for loitering. Two of my best animals, and he walks up and fires them! Has this place gone crazy? What happened to the conditions of the contract?

"Sure I know, we'll grieve it and we'll win, but in the meantime I have my two best workers off the job. Do you know how hard it is to keep good skilled labor? They can both have others job tomorrow, and they will. They told me this place wasn't worth the grief, they're glad to go." Muley slammed his hoof on the table under Liz's nose. "We've had nothing but trouble since you and your tigers showed up. I don't know which way is up anymore. "

Liz was about to speak, but Muley wasn't finished.

"Don't give me your corporate party line, lady. Don't waste my time. If you want to get my attention, get my workers back before I lose them. Get that damned Beaver out of my life." Muley's nose was within an inch of Liz's.

"This is distressing. I'll resolve this before I leave today. Ask your workers not to take action until I've had time to look into the matter."

"You have until the end of today, period. It'll be hard for me to hold my workers off that long. I want something done about Beaver."

"While you're looking into things, check the temporary lodging for the snakes," said Arnold, the groundskeeper. "Beaver has them in a tent near the picnic grounds. He's clearing away their old building. The snakes are plenty mad about the temporary quarters. I don't blame them."

He paused for breath. "Now they're really acting up. Barney Boa was so mad he ate a customer's picnic basket just this morning. Scared the family half to death. I'm telling you, lady, you've got one helluva mess on your hands."

"I had no idea any of this was going on. These conditions must be corrected immediately. We'll have to postpone this meeting." She was gone in a flash with Charlie right behind her.

"I'm going to commandeer your office for awhile, Charlie. I need to make calls back to headquarters. Find Beaver, and bring him to your office immediately." She paused. "Have the workers clear the picnic area and rope it off. We don't want snakes terrorizing the customers."

"Ms. Lioness," Jane called as Liz sped down the hall. "May I have a word with you?"

"Not now. I'm in a rush."

Liz was on the phone to Zoolandia within seconds. When she hung up a long time later, she noticed Charlie standing there.

"Where's Beaver?" Liz asked.

"I don't know, Liz. I looked everywhere, and no one knows where he is."

"Is it unusual for him to disappear like that?"

"I'm sure he'll show up eventually. Let's not worry prematurely."

"Okay, we'll wait for a while and see. What have you done about the picnic area?"

"That's a bigger problem than I thought. The snakes are refusing to go back to the tent."

"Who is responsible for the snakes?"

"Morley Mongoose manages the snakehouse, and he's there now."

"I talked to Ted Tiger and he said the snakehouse wasn't scheduled to be torn down until the snakes were transferred out."

"Transferred? Where are they going?"

"Oh, I forgot you wouldn't know. Theme parks don't employ exhibit snakes. We plan to employ them at the exotic animal farm."

Charlie dropped into his chair.

"How many more surprises are we in for, Liz?"

Liz ignored the question.

"Ted is making arrangements to transfer the snakes immediately. In the meantime, have Morley find more appropriate accommodations for them. And send Muley here, I need to get this other mess straightened out right away."

Charlie felt like a gofer with Liz making all the decisions.

Liz was gathering her thoughts when Jane walked in.

"Ms. Lioness, I'd like a word with you."

"Is this something that can wait? I'm very busy at the moment."

"It will only take a minute."

"Please make it brief."

"My name is Jane Porcupine. I'm the manager of the purchasing department."

"I know."

"I've been told by a reliable source that I'm getting a significant promotion. It's about time women had an opportunity to climb corporate ladders."

"I'm sorry, Jane. I don't know anything about a promotion for you. Where did you get this information?"

"It's all over the zoo. Everyone knows about it." Jane's voice rose.

"It's too bad you had your hopes up for nothing, Jane. There are no promotions planned for you at this time."

"You're wrong! I heard it myself from a reliable source."

"Unfortunately, your source isn't reliable. I'm sorry."

"I don't believe a word you've said! I'll call headquarters myself."

Jane passed Duane Beaver as she rushed angrily from the room.

"I understand you were looking for me, ma'am?"

"Yes, Duane, I am. Where have you been? We looked all over the zoo."

"I made a special run into town for machine parts."

"That's a good example of the problem we're having with you, Duane. You either go around the accepted procedures or you ignore them entirely."

"I'm sorry, ma'am, I don't know what you're referring to."

"Duane, you're in such a hurry to succeed that you're falling all over yourself. Zoolandia can't tolerate this sort of thing. It's imperative for accounting to have the proper paperwork for purchases."

"But, ma'am, I've got a tight schedule and several days of waiting for parts is unacceptable."

"You heard me. The subject is closed. There are other two incidents with serious ramifications I want to discuss. The first one is the snakehouse. You've razed it a month ahead of schedule."

"Yes, it was in the way."

"Duane, that schedule was for a purpose. You can't tear down the snakehouse without alternate accommodations for the snakes."

"I found a place for them. They're in the tent near the picnic area."

"A tent was not designed to house snakes, Duane. It's degrading. No wonder they're angry."

"I'm really sorry, ma'am. I never meant to cause all of this trouble."

"That's not all, Duane. Muley tells me you fired two of his workers today."

"Yes I did." Duane sat up straight. "I can't tolerate workers loitering on the job. I warned them and they ignored my warning."

"Did you put the warnings in writing, Duane?"

"No, but don't worry. They heard me all right."

"That's not the point. We have a regular discipline procedure we follow with union workers. We'll have to reinstate them."

"You can't do that. I'll be the laughing stock of the zoo."

"We have no choice. Furthermore, it's about time you became aware of the consequences of your behavior. You've violated contractual items and set up an unnecessarily adversarial environment. That's just the sort of thing that stirs up the militant union members. You're to treat the workers well, follow the discipline procedure, and follow the construction schedule. Is that clear?"

"Yes, ma'am. Thanks for the warning."

"Call Ted Tiger right away, and go over your progress with him. He has no idea what's been done."

Duane had hardly left when Charlie came walking in.

"Big Al Boa is missing. Morley is out looking for him. We think he's hiding in the weeds by the picnic area. We could have more trouble."

Liz shrugged in exasperation.

"I've talked to Duane. Put the workers back on the payroll, and be sure they get paid for today."

"I'll get on it. What should we do about the union rep meeting?"

"It will have to wait until the next meeting time. The rest of my day is completely scheduled."

• • •

When Liz came for the next union meeting, Mike Tiger came with her to look things over and check on progress. He hadn't informed anyone he was coming and when he walked into Luke's office in the morning, Luke wasn't there.

"Oh, Mr. Tiger, it's you," said Wendy. "Can I get you a cup of coffee. There's a pot freshly brewed down the hall."

"Thanks. That would hit the spot."

Wendy headed out the door and suddenly stopped.

"Mr. Tiger, Luke has a Chamber of Commerce breakfast meeting. He won't be in until after nine."

"That's all right, Wendy, I'll just wait."

Wendy returned with the coffee and set it down carefully on the desk. She turned to leave.

"I understand you're taking the voluntary retirement, Wendy."

"Yes, I'll be leaving in a few weeks."

"You don't sound happy."

"This job is all I have, Mr. Tiger. I hate to leave it like this."

"If you hate to leave it, why are you?"

"I have no choice."

"Are you taking the retirement plan because you're afraid you'll be fired if you don't?"

"Yes, that's about it." A tear rolled down her cheek.

"Excuse me, sir, I didn't mean to cry." She scurried out of the office to the females' latrine.

By the time Luke arrived at his office, Wendy was at her desk.

"Mike, how long have you been here? I had a meeting this morning or I would have been here sooner."

"It's all right, Luke. I had a chance to chat with Wendy while I was waiting for you. She seems pretty upset about retiring next month."

"She gets upset about everything."

"She thinks she has to take this retirement or you'll force her out."

"I suggested she consider retiring since she hasn't been cutting it lately."

"Were you planning to fire her, Luke?"

"I don't have to. She's retiring."

"If she hadn't taken the plan, what justification would you have to fire her, Luke?"

"What difference does it make now? She's taking the plan. I don't know what you're getting at."

"What I'm getting at is this. She's retiring because she thinks she'll get fired otherwise."

"Do you expect me to keep incompetent workers?"

"No."

Silence.

"Well, then what's the problem?"

"Do you have some problem with older workers? This is the third time I've seen you antagonize an older worker. First Roy Raccoon, then Ben Bear, now Wendy."

"What's wrong with expecting people to do their jobs? Should I make extra allowances for animals who are old and can no longer carry their weight?"

"Luke, I warn you, you're on dangerous turf. I've told you before and I'm telling you again, Zoolandia sometimes makes hard business decisions, but we're not cruel."

"You've got this all turned around, Mike. This is a voluntary program. I didn't force her to sign up."

"Yes, you did. And I'm going to rectify that right now. She's going to be your secretary for a long time, Luke. Do I make myself clear?"

Luke wasn't fooled by the softness of Mike's voice.

"Of course, of course, Mike. I can see it might have seemed insensitive. I'll tell Wendy myself that we'd like her to stay on as long as she wants."

"Good. Now you and I have business to conduct before I meet Liz for lunch. She's meeting with the union reps, and I want to get an update as soon as it's over." Mike opened his briefcase and pulled out some papers.

"According to the report Millie Pigeon sent in, fifteen animals are taking early retirement, actually fourteen now. Based on the revenue of this zoo, we've determined to cut another thirty-five salaried animals."

"We're barely able to keep things going with the animals we have now," Luke broke in.

"I'll give you two weeks to put together a plan to reach the numbers we want."

"This isn't going to make me popular with the animals, Mike."

"It's not the acting president's job to be popular."

Mike picked up a piece of paper and handed it to Luke.

"This memo will go out over your signature. It announces an immediate salary freeze. It goes to all non-union employees."

Luke looked at the memo as Mike left.

Mike and Liz planned to meet at the Happy Holiday Hotel restaurant for lunch. When he got there she was waiting .

"How did it go, Liz?"

"Things are really heating up. It was a shouting match. The animals are frustrated. They say the zoo is so torn up they can't accommodate the customers, and they're taking heavy abuse from customers for things beyond their control."

"Are they the usual change frustrations or is it something more serious?"

"Some of both. We've torn up this zoo much more severely than most. I'm wondering whether we should have closed down for a period. There are legitimate safety concerns. Muley said the barriers around construction sites are insufficient. With so many children visiting the zoo, one could sneak into a construction site and be seriously hurt."

"The union knows a layoff is coming," she continued. "All the talk in the world about a bright future won't fool them. They're demanding equity in the company in exchange for the sacrifices the company will demand. Julia Peacock made an impassioned plea to have the animals become a real part of the corporation by making them stockholders. Of course, that's not an option in our takeover procedure, but it's an interesting suggestion."

"What do you think of Julia, Liz?"

"I like her. She's articulate and bright, not afraid to take a tough stand."

"Do you think she'd be interested in moving to a corporate position in Theatrical Productions?"

"I don't know. What an idea, Mike. If she'd go, she'd be a smashing success."

"We'd have to handle it carefully. The unions will scream bloody murder if they think we're trying to buy her off. Maybe we'd better sit on the idea for a while. Anything else of interest?"

"They asked me about survival of their union after the acquisition. They weren't happy when I told them Zoolandia's policy was not to interfere in union business. I said we'd have transition agreements with each union until they can all be folded into one through elections. They don't have the votes to win the election, and they know it.

"We're meeting in two weeks, and the transition agreement will be the first agenda item." Liz paused a moment, deep in thought.

"I'm concerned about morale, especially when the word gets out about the salary freeze," said Mike.

"All we can do now is keep the lines of communication open. Meeting again in two weeks is a good idea. I've been thinking I should come to town more often for management meetings."

"What's on your schedule this afternoon, Liz?" Mike asked as they left the restaurant.

"I'm going to talk to Nurse Goat. Then I have to remind Hamilton Hog that he is to be fully automated at the end of this week."

"Sounds like a full afternoon. How about if we just meet in time for our flight?"

"Fine, see you then."

Mike went straight to Luke's office after lunch.

"Hi, Mike. Did you have a nice lunch?"

"It was all right, thanks. Some things came up in the union rep meeting that I want to discuss with you. Have you been watching Beaver's operation?"

"Well, no, not exactly. I mean he tells me when I see him that everything is going well. As a matter of fact, he told me he's ahead of schedule on the construction."

"That's the problem. Tell me, Luke, do you have staff meetings?"

"I prefer to meet with my staff individually whenever I think it's necessary."

"Is that on a regular basis?"

"No."

"That's not good enough. You're to bring your staff together at least once a week. There's just no other way to be certain you know what's going on around here."

"I didn't think staff meetings were necessary. Ewald's were ice cream socials, and I personally hated them."

"You may be right about Ewald's staff meetings. They shouldn't be social affairs. Keep the time to a minimum. But make certain every one of your staff members keeps you up to date on what they're doing."

Mike continued.

"You're right about Duane being ahead of schedule. He's so far ahead he has created all kinds of problems."

Liz knocked and came in.

"We have another crisis on our hands, Mike. I was just talking to Hamilton Hog about the automation process, and he went completely berserk. He was squealing and beating his hooves on the desk. It was frightening. I was afraid he was having a heart attack. Someone called Nurse Goat, and she was there in a flash. She gave him a sedative, and had him carried to her office. It's an anxiety attack, not a heart attack, according to her. She called it another fine example of the effects of Zoolandia's takeover. Then she asked me how many more animals we had to kill or break before we'd go away."

"Excuse me."

Everyone looked up to see Sarah Giraffe in the doorway.

"I just heard about Hamilton, and I knew I'd better come talk to you."

"Come in, Sarah."

"I'll just be a minute. I can explain Ham's reaction to your mention of the automation project, Ms. Lioness. He doesn't know anything about it, really. Doing constant budget edits has kept him under such stress he's been delegating everything else to me. I knew about the switchover this weekend. Ham didn't. I didn't want to add to his worries. Now I see it would have been better to tell him. I feel terrible."

"You were both wrong. You should have told him and he should have asked."

"I intended to tell Ham tomorrow morning. We're all set to go and it's not a problem. But he didn't know that either."

It was time to leave for the airport when the young goat from Nurse's office knocked on Luke's door. Liz recognized her instantly and called her in.

"What can we do for you?" Liz could see that the goat was very nervous.

"I have two messages from Nurse," she said as she started to cry.

Everyone sat still, hardly breathing. Finally she continued.

"The first message is that Mr. Hog is still incoherent, and Nurse has made arrangements for him to be admitted to the State Animal Hospital. She expects he'll be unable to work for several months. His family is on the way to the hospital. They'll meet Mr. Hog and Nurse there."

She paused as if she couldn't bring herself to give them the second message. Finally, she handed Mike a letter, and before anyone could say a word, she was gone.

Mike looked at the letter. It was Nurse's letter of resignation, effective immediately.

5

Autumn arrived; children returned to school, and zoo attendance declined, a blessing since the zoo was almost at a standstill. It looked like a combat zone. The few animal exhibits still open were surrounded by construction and mud.

Willy Weasel was the only animal in high spirits. He darted about, talking to one group of animals after another. But business at the souvenir shop was dead, and many afternoons he closed himself in his office.

News of the layoff had traveled through the zoo like the wind. Word had it that Luke and his staff were evaluating employees and would make a decision about which would stay or go. The latest rumor had the go number at well over seventy-five.

Happy Valley had became a battleground for BUZWA (Brotherhood of United Zoological Workers Amalgamated), the union representing Happy Valley workers, and ZAP (Zoological Association of Professionals), the union representing Zoolandia workers. Both unions were fighting for sole representation of the combined work force. The campaign heated up quickly and brochures and buttons blanketed the zoo. Happy Valley animals were confused and torn. BUZWA and ZAP were old rivals, and this was the culmination of a long line of skirmishes. ZAP was rapidly eroding BUZWA's national membership, and Happy Valley became the scene for a potential showdown.

Happy Valley union reps were overwhelmed with information and advice. Merging the seniority lists of a little zoo like Happy Valley with a conglomerate like Zoolandia favored the Zoolandia animals. Happy Valley animals worried about being forced to other zoos and about their families being uprooted. Nerves were frayed, and tempers flared.

Construction fell behind schedule. No matter how much Duane cajoled or screamed, the animals didn't move. Muley's workers lost equipment and materials that didn't turn up for days. They taunted Duane, reminding him they were going by the contract..

Luke started having weekly Monday morning staff meetings, at which he whipped through his agenda. Radar Dolphin had returned from his training at Zoolandia headquarters. He attended the staff meetings and was rather mysterious about his new job.

Staff reductions took up a great deal of time in the first two meetings. First, staff members pointed at others as better able to take cuts. Duane argued that he needed all his workers to meet the slipping construction schedule while Carl Crocodile, vice president of Operations, claimed he could make a 30-percent cut if Duane's organization reported to him. Duane came out of his chair, waving his arms, and yelling at Carl. Luke threatened to make the decisions himself if the bickering didn't stop. He demanded separate meetings to identify the 15 percent each would cut. An across-the-board approach was the only way manageable, he thought—except for Radar Dolphin's department, which Zoolandia had exempted from cuts.

• • •

Mike and Liz noticed significant changes on their next visit. Union campaign posters were everywhere. With fewer customers, the zoo was much quieter. But the change in the animals themselves was the greatest. They kept their eyes downcast, and their movements were slow.

"Looks like we'd better move things along as fast as possible, Liz. The animals look depressed."

"Yes. I'm worried about what I see."

"It's not unusual in an acquisition, but it's not a condition to be prolonged."

Luke was prepared when Mike arrived at his office. He had a carafe of coffee and a plate of assorted Danish rolls. His office was shining. He couldn't trust Sweeper to clean it well enough, so he had come in early to spruce it up himself. No more slip-ups for Luke, no sir. Even Wendy looked especially nice today. She was her perky old self, pecking away at the typewriter.

"Good morning, Mr. Tiger," she chirped as Mike came through.

"Morning, Wendy."

Mike walked into Luke's office. He was amused at Luke's obvious preparations for his visit.

"Morning, Luke."

"Welcome, Mike. I've been waiting for you. We've been doing a lot of good work since your last visit. I think you'll like what you hear."

"Good. Let's get right down to business. I expect we have a full slate."

Luke presented his list of cuts to Mike. Thirty-five animals were to be laid off. As Mike scanned the list, he noticed a large number of older workers.

"We'll have to do some bumping, Luke. Looks like quite a few older workers on the list."

"What? Bumping? If they no longer have a position, they go."

"Not if they're qualified to do something a less senior animal is doing. Zoolandia can't afford an age discrimination suit."

"There are some pretty young animals in Marketing. Why don't we make some cuts there?"

"Marketing is not to be touched, Luke. I thought that was clear. Do you have organization charts for all of your staff?"

"I think so. I left that to Wendy. I'll ask her to get right on it."

In a moment he returned with the charts.

"She's been keeping them up to date all along. We're in business." Luke seemed half surprised.

"Good. Let's take a look. By the end of the day, I want the list finalized. We'll notify them next week and put them into the Zoolandia outplacement procedure immediately."

"What's that?"

"It's a series of steps to help laid-off animals cope with their grief and anger and secure new positions. I'll give you a complete rundown. We'll bring outplacement experts from headquarters."

Mike poured a cup of coffee, then continued.

"What you and I have to work out now is notification procedure and timing. I want them notified next Thursday. They will be relieved of job responsibilities immediately but remain on the payroll during the four weeks of outplacement. Charlie Fox and Millie Pigeon will do the exit interviews, and Zoolandia well do the rest. We'll need a building or a floor of a building dedicated to outplacement. We don't want laid-off animals wandering through the working areas. It's too distracting."

"We're a bit short on buildings, Mike. Every one is in the process of going up or down."

"I'll check with Duane. It's possible we can set up something temporary in the restaurant pit. I'd hate to take over the Watering Hole, but if we have to we will."

"That would be dangerous. I've been feeling an undercurrent of hostility among the animals."

"Do you have any idea who the ringleaders might be?"

"No. I don't hear many rumors."

"Can you think of anyone who might be willing to talk about it?"

"Not at the moment. Duane thinks Muley's workers are the troublemakers."

Later that morning Mike had an opportunity to talk to Wendy. He asked her the same questions.

"Wendy, I know I'm putting you in a spot, and I've got to ask you to trust me. The future of Happy Valley is on the line here, and you may be able to help save it."

Wendy was torn. Jane was a longtime, loyal friend, and she had promised to say nothing.

"Mr. Tiger, I'd really like to help you. But don't you see? These are my friends. I can't just turn on them like that."

"I understand, Wendy. It's a tough decision, and I respect your dilemma. Your loyalty should be to Zoolandia and all the loyal animals."

"Well, I don't know much except what Jane Porcupine told me. Evidently Willy Weasel is enlisting animals in a scheme to take the zoo back from Zoolandia. He has been making some wild and frightening accusations about Roy's death. And he made a similar claim about Hamilton. I don't know much more."

Wendy looked through her desk drawer.

"Here's something that may be connected. I've noticed that Willy's extension has a large number of long-distance calls over the past two weeks."

"Can I see the log, Wendy?" Mike looked it over. "This is a great piece of detective work. Thanks. Do you think your friend Jane is involved with Willy?"

Wendy averted her eyes and hesitated.

"I don't know, Mr. Tiger. She's been approached. She's very bitter about not getting a promotion from Zoolandia. She's feeling cheated and embarrassed. She may not be a part of the scheme, Mr. Tiger, but she won't give you any help either. Of that, I'm certain."

Mike headed for the cafeteria to meet Liz for lunch. His morning had been productive. He would have Willy's phone calls traced.

"I wonder what all that nonsense about Raccoon and Hog was about," he wondered to himself.

Liz's morning with the unions was intense. The animals became more aggressive as their anger spiraled. She made a mental note to move the meetings from the Watering Hole to a more neutral place.

Employee demands for equity in the company had heated up. They wanted assurance that they wouldn't be forced to move to other zoos.

They would give no concessions, and they would go by the letter of their contracts. No overtime, and they didn't give a damn how things got done. Everything was such a mess, they said, and it was beyond their capability to straighten it out. Neither were they about to try.

Grinder Monkey had been extremely hostile to Liz.

"I understand Zoolandia Theme Parks have monorails not trams. I suppose you'll just say thanks for all of your past loyalty and good work, and now kiss off." He had leapt onto the table, hunched in front of her.

"You're right, Mr. Monkey. There are monorails at theme parks. I'm not going to deny reality. The switch will be dealt with through the union contract negotiating procedures. It's nothing you and I can decide here. I'm here to help ease the transition and answer questions."

"And haven't you done a fine job of that?" Grinder asked sarcastically. "If you ease it any more, we'll all be in the loony bin or out of a job."

"What I'm not here for is abuse. Zoolandia wants a smooth transition. We've converted many zoos into theme parks successfully. There's always a certain amount of turmoil, and you're no different from others. It all gets worked through if all parties can cooperate."

"Cooperate, my ass. Lady, we have nothing to gain by cooperating. You've shown us nothing to indicate otherwise. I don't see any need for more meetings," Muley brayed.

"Wait, Muley. Let's not act too hastily," said Julia. "Let's hold open the possibility of meeting again."

"Not if we're just going to have more meetings where she feeds us the party bullshit. If we have something we want to meet about, then let's meet. Otherwise, I'm not going to be there. It's not part of my job description."

"I'll leave it up to you to call the next meeting," Liz began. "Before we end this meeting, I'd like to offer some thoughts for consideration. You've mentioned your fear of layoffs. It's possible you can head them off by coming up with alternatives. How about reduced work hours? Zoolandia is always willing to look at proposals that are in the best interest of the company and the workers."

Liz sensed their hostility, but she was determined to finish.

"The other important issue is the slipping construction schedule. Zoolandia has a set schedule and we'll meet it no matter what. I know you're going by the letter of your contract, and we can't force you to do otherwise—nor would we. But we may be forced to cancel some vacations."

The animals had volunteered to take vacations before or after the busiest time of the year, summer. The majority planned for fall, when most resorts were still open.

"You can't do that!" exploded Muley.

"Read your contract. We can and will if we have to."

"Well, I've made vacation plans and I'm going. Period."

"If we cancel vacations and you decide to go anyway, we'll have grounds for termination."

"The way I feel now, that suits me fine. You can take this job and shove it!"

"If you are trying to resign, I'd suggest you put it in writing. I'd also suggest you cool down and think about it first. Once you submit a resignation, it's final. Make no mistake about that." Liz looked around the room.

"I really don't see much point in continuing this meeting. I'll wait to hear from you about whether we should meet. If not, we'll start contract negotiations immediately after the union elections."

• • •

Mike and Liz spent the afternoon dropping in unofficially to talk to animals. Reaction was mixed—from pleasantly surprised to openly hostile. The two treated all the animals alike, without avoiding the angry ones. It was a familiar drill for them both.

Mike made a point of checking on Sarah Giraffe. He found her in her office working on the budget. Engrossed in her work, she was startled when he spoke.

"Oh, excuse me. I didn't see you coming. I heard you and Liz were here today. It's nice of you to stop by," she said.

"I wanted to check with you and see how it's going. In this acting position, you've taken on a heavy load. I'm concerned we don't overdo it. We can't afford another incident like Hamilton."

"Oh, don't worry. The workers have picked up the slack. I'm proud of them, actually. And the automated system makes the budget edits much easier."

"About these budget edits. How often do you make them?"

"For awhile, Luke had Ham making them daily. Now I'm giving Luke weekly edits. He doesn't always like my answer—I don't always like it either—but he accepts it."

"Good. You don't need any unnecessary work. How is this layoff going to affect you?"

Sarah frowned. "It's going to hurt, but I think I've got it worked out. We have some bright and promising new accounting clerks who will go. I know they can get jobs without much problem, but I just hate to lose them."

"Layoffs are always hard, and it seems the young animals take the brunt of it. I'm hoping we can recover from this quickly enough to hire some of them back soon."

"I'm afraid it will be too late for these workers. They'll be on another job in no time."

"Have you had much contact with Jane Porcupine? I'm wondering how she's doing."

Sarah looked off into space for a long time before she answered.

"I don't know exactly what you're asking. I've always managed to get what I need from Jane."

"Do you think she'd be involved in any type of sabotage of the company?"

Sarah eyes widened.

"My guess would be no. She needs her job too much to jeopardize it. Not that she wouldn't like to. She's been pretty openly bitter. Apparently she thought she was in for a big promotion."

Mike had his answer. Chances were Jane was not involved in Willy's scheme. His next stop was to see Radar Dolphin, whom he didn't know much about. Radar was middle-aged, full of fun. Below his jolly exterior was a sound and steady temperament. Mike found Radar in his office, working on a marketing plan. He hummed as he worked.

"Hi, Radar. How's it going?"

"Oh, hi, Mike. It's good to see you. Sit down. Have I got news for you!"

Mike sat down. Radar opened a folder and began pulling out one mock-up brochure after another.

"When this place is ready to kick off the theme park marketing plan, I've got enough ideas finished to keep us in business for ten years. The convention center brochure is complete, we've about got the newspaper ad campaign wrapped up, and I've been talking to the local TV and radio stations. All I need is word from you to kick it off, and we're in business."

Mike liked what he saw. All the materials adhered to the Zoolandia guidelines and showed fresh creativity.

"This is all superb, Radar."

"Thanks, Mike. Actually my only concern is that we don't launch this campaign so soon or so heavy that the animals react badly. They're already nervous about all the changes."

"I understand your concern, Radar, but the zoo has been losing money right along. Zoolandia has been pouring in capital investment and is impatient for revenue. We'll just have to manage as best we can when they turn on the marketing program."

"I figured you were going to say that, Mike. Well, I've been working to get my staff ready. I plan to have them helping with the transition wherever they can. They're a good bunch, and they'll break their necks working."

"I'm sure you're right. Keep up the good work."

Mike left Radar's office, humming the same tune as Radar.

• • •

When Mike and Liz arrived back at Zoolandia Headquarters, Mike put in a call to the head of Security. Within hours Willy's activities were under full investigation. Mike received a list of the long-distance phone calls Willy had made. Several were to vendors—odd because he was not authorized to contact them directly. A couple were to residences in Atlantic City, New Jersey. Those were puzzling, too. The next few on the list were not puzzling at all. Willy had called the federal Occupational Safety and Health Administration (OSHA), the national headquarters of American Society for the Prevention of Cruelty to Animals (ASPCA), the Justice Department Antitrust Division, and the State Health Commissioner's office.

Mike made a whistling sound.

"My my. Willy certainly has been busy."

It wasn't a matter of whether Willy had done any damage, but a question of how much. Security would make the decision on this one, with no moves until the investigation was complete. Mike was impatient. Time was crucial.

• • •

Preparations for the Happy Valley layoff began immediately. Charlie and Millie would conduct simultaneous group exit interviews. They found two rooms in the restaurant area that would provide privacy and comfort. Tables and chairs were rented for the four-week period, computer terminals were installed for resume writing, phones were installed with unlimited access to long distance, and stationery supplies were ordered. Millie Pigeon put together benefit packages to be distributed to each laid-off employee. Maynard Skunk's payroll department calculated severance pay and prepared checks. When the layoff day arrived, everything was complete.

Charlie had instructed the managers to notify affected employees first thing Thursday morning, then send them to the restaurant area.

Then they were to reassure the remaining workers, who would be picking up extra duties. Charlie reminded the managers that the workers who stay would need to understand their new duties and how changes would affect them.

The animals showing up for exit interviews had a glazed look of disbelief. This couldn't be happening to them. It must be some kind of mistake. They had been a part of Happy Valley, and they had expected to retire from here. They sat down quickly, with little conversation. A few cried quietly as they waited for the session to begin. Some of the newer workers joked about taking time off to kick back and enjoy their freedom. They hadn't been with Happy Valley long, and at least on the surface, they were optimistic about finding other jobs. In most cases their optimism was well founded. But even the young ones quieted when they saw obvious pain on the faces of senior workers.

Charlie and Millie began the sessions with brief acknowledgements of how difficult this time was for the workers. They moved right into assurances that laid-off workers would be provided a great deal of assistance. They went over a four-week schedule so the workers would know what to expect and to give them a sense of purpose. Finally, they went over necessary documents and distributed checks. It was about as much as the employees could manage.

As Charlie headed for his office afterward, trouble began. Animals started running about, shouting obscenities, smashing and overturning furniture.

"What the hell's going on?" he wondered, at first frozen on the spot. He'd never experienced anything like this before. Given the looks in the eyes of some of the animals, he decided he'd best talk to Radar.

Charlie was out of breath by the time he reached the administration building. He had to bang on the door and tell them who he was before they let him in. Some of the workers had barricaded the door against the rioters.

"What the hell is going on out there?"

"We didn't get the paychecks out today," Scott Skunk answered. We were swamped by the severance checks, and the system couldn't handle paychecks at the same time."

"You mean to tell me the animals didn't get paid today?"

"That's about it. Don't look at me. It's not our fault. I don't see how they expected us to get all that done. We're not miracle workers."

"Now don't get excited. Just tell me what you know."

"Well, first thing we know, Maynard came out of his office and said we had miscalculated the severance checks. He went running over to the restaurant area to tell you, but you were already gone. Now we have to figure a way to get all those checks back. We hardly had a chance to think about that, when the damned secretaries started showing up for paychecks. When they found out we didn't have the checks done, they went back and incited a riot."

"I hardly think the secretaries incited a riot, Scott. Well, it doesn't matter much now, does it? Just keep this door closed till it passes. Once tempers flare, there's no telling how far it will go."

Charlie started for his office. He could feel the angry heat traveling up his body.

"I planned today down to the gnat's eyebrow. They screw up the severance pay, plus the workers don't get their paychecks. They're not going to lay this one on me!" he thought.

When Charlie reached his office, he slammed the door shut and picked up the phone. He was going to talk to Liz and get a few things straight. Enough was enough. His call went through, but he was unprepared for the response when he asked for Liz.

"I'm sorry, Mr. Fox, Ms. Lioness is no longer employed by this division."

"What do you mean, she's no longer employed by this division?" Charlie could feel his temples pounding.

"She has accepted a position as vice president of Human Resources with the Exotic Animal Ranch Division."

"When did she leave?" Charlie was still trying to absorb the news.

"Actually, her last official day is tomorrow, but she packed up her desk and turned it over to Larry Lion a day early."

"Larry Lion is replacing her?" Charlie couldn't believe it. Larry was a cub who had little, if any, labor relations experience.

"Yes, Mr. Fox. Can I put you through?"

"No thanks." Charlie hung up. All of this time he had been trying to impress Liz, and for what? She was gone just like that. He began to think about his relationship with the Happy Valley animals as he sat looking out the window watching them running through the zoo. They were not a bad bunch. Mostly they wanted the zoo to succeed, too.

Since Zoolandia had taken over, everything had changed. His relationships with just about everyone had deteriorated. And look what happened to the unions. ZAP moved in and demanded an election. The animals were about to be swallowed up in a shoot-out between two national unions. It was time someone stood up for Happy Valley. He didn't see anyone else in line for the job.

• • •

Sarah was working on the budget when she heard the noise outside. She took one look, decided things were beyond control, and called the local police. Several squad cars arrived, then sent for the Animal Guard. The guards arrived in large troop carriers, quickly restored order, and sent everyone home. A small guard contingent would be watching the zoo overnight.

• • •

The next morning Duane and his supervisors assessed the damage, which appeared extensive. Debris was scattered everywhere. Construction vehicles were overturned, new walls were spray-painted with graffiti, Sheldon's classroom was completely demolished, all the portable toilets were turned over, and windows were broken, the glass scattered about.

Duane suspended all construction and set workers to cleaning up the mess. He walked around, personally checking their progress, unable to conceal his anger and frustration. The angrier Beaver got, the better the workers liked it.

"Look at the S.O.B., he's practically lathering at the mouth," one mule brayed. They all laughed and snorted. This was sweet revenge. The riot was worth it just to see Beaver in a hopeless rage.

• • •

The laid-off workers began reporting for their first outplacement sessions in the restaurant area. The animals gathered around tables of coffee and rolls set up outside the meeting rooms. They talked about how it was with their families. Some were pleasantly surprised by the positive reactions. Others seemed even more frightened than the day before.

Zoolandia sent eight professional outplacement counselors and three administrative support animals for the four weeks. They were well aware they would be the target of the laid-off workers' anger. They were prepared to maintain empathy and support while helping the animals find new employment.

• • •

Charlie had spent a sleepless night, tossing and turning over ideas in his mind. When he arrived at work Friday morning, he moved into action, calling on Julia first.

"Julia, I've got some important things I need to talk to you about."

"I'm sure you do, Charlie. Things are in a bit of a mess just now." Her nerves frayed, Julia was prepared for a fight.

"I warned you when Sheldon's classroom was damaged, Charlie. You just wouldn't listen. I hate what happened here. It does something terrible to the animals too, you know. This isn't like them."

Charlie managed to get a word in.

"Julia, I'm not here to fight. I'm as upset as you are."

"Well, then. What do you want?"

"First of all, I called Zoolandia to talk to Liz. I was going to tell her about the paychecks and what a mess that created here. I wanted to tell her that Zoolandia had put an impossible burden on Maynard. It's no wonder he didn't get the checks out." Charlie stopped a moment to think. Then he got up and paced around the room.

"I didn't talk to Liz, Julia. Do you know why?" Charlie swung around and looked at Julia. Before she could answer, he continued. "I'll tell you why. Because she's no longer there! Apparently she's taken a big promotion in a different division." Charlie was pacing again. He lit another cigarette.

"This will really kill you, Julia. Do you know who is replacing her? Larry Lion, for God's sake. He's just a wet-behind-the-ears cub with almost no experience. I'd be a damned sight better than Larry. Well, screw them. I don't need their lousy job."

Julia watched Charlie. She felt sorry for him.

"I can handle Larry. He's no match for me. And I've got some idea of how I can help the union reps, too. I'm sick of seeing Happy Valley get raped. We've got rights, and we can stand up for them," he said.

"Charlie, if you want to talk about helping the unions, I don't think there's an animal alive who wouldn't be willing to listen. Do you have something specific in mind?"

"Yes. As a matter of fact, I do. For starters, let's take Zoolandia up on their offer to visit theme parks. The more we know about how they are run, the better off we are. I'm not sure it makes sense for me to go on these visits with you, but one way or another I'm going to do the same thing. We need to know what we're dealing with here."

"Great idea, Charlie. I suppose you want me to sell it to the union reps?"

"They'd listen to you, Julia. Right now I think anything I said would be suspect." He paused a minute, then managed a wry smile.

"I mean more suspect than usual."

Julia smiled, too.

"Your standing isn't the greatest, Charlie. The animals think you've been struck dumb lately. Liz has been doing all the talking." She hurried on.

"In any case, you're right. We need information badly, and visiting theme parks is the best answer. I don't know whether the union treasury can afford too many trips. We'll have to see about that."

Someone Is Buying the Zoo 67

When Charlie got back to his office he put in a call to Larry Lion. He had rehearsed this conversation several times during the night.

"Larry, Charlie Fox here. I understand you have replaced Liz Lioness. Congratulations and good luck."

"Thanks, Charlie. I appreciate the support. I was going to call you on Monday when I'm officially in the job. Since you've called today, let's get right down to work." Larry was all business.

"That's fine with me, Larry. That's why I'm calling. Liz mentioned to the union reps that they should visit some of the theme parks. That's an excellent idea, and the union reps are interested in getting some visits lined up. I'd like to do the same thing. If I'm going to be negotiating contracts, I need a better idea of what the theme parks are like."

"Hold on Charlie. Not so fast. We have something more urgent to talk about than theme park visits. I understand there was a riot at your zoo yesterday. The word is the exit interview process wasn't handled well. Is that right?"

"Only half your information is correct. There was a riot here, but the cause can be laid on your doorstep, Larry. You animals sit at headquarters and issue orders that are impossible. Then you call back here and chew us out for the consequences." Charlie's voice had taken a sharp edge, and he reminded himself to stay cool.

"The exit interviews went off without a hitch. No one could have done a better job."

"Now listen, Charlie. I'm not going to have you talking to me like that. You'd better get straight about who's in charge here."

"I'm not questioning your authority, Larry. What I am saying is that Zoolandia has been a big factor in our problems. You need to listen more closely to what's happening here and give us more freedom to manage events. Maynard's payroll system isn't equipped to issue severance and payroll checks at the same time. If you had asked, you wouldn't have created this mess."

"That was a sound decision, one I would make again."

"Look, Larry, we can argue this forever and never agree. I don't see much point to it. What I want is to make arrangements to visit theme parks and have the union reps do the same. Now, is that a problem for you or not?"

When Charlie and Larry hung up, they had agreed to Charlie's plan. Charlie headed for Radar Dolphin's office.

"Hey, Fox. Glad you dragged your tail over here. Have a seat."

Charlie sat down gratefully.

"Things are getting out of hand around here, Radar. You couldn't have missed the riot yesterday."

"Hardly. The noise alone was enough to wake the dead. Heard it was over paychecks."

"Well, it was and it wasn't. Just the straw that broke the camel's back. Things haven't been right here since Zoolandia took over. I've just begun to realize that I can act as an employee advocate to the corporation and head off more trouble. The corporation needs someone like me to tell them when they're off base."

"Charlie, I'm speechless. Now, tell me, where's the hook?"

"No kidding, Radar, I mean it. There's no hook. I've just gotten off the hook, now that I think of it. I've been trying to work a promotion to corporate headquarters, and I've been angling with Liz Lioness to get it. Now she's been promoted to another division. I've kissed a corporate job good-bye, and I want to help the animals."

"Good for you. Now I imagine there is some part for me in this change of heart. Am I right?"

"Right, as usual. I want to find out as much as I can about what's in store for the animals. With that, we can prepare for it. I've already made arrangements for union reps to visit theme parks, and I'm going to go see them myself. I have a feeling you can give me a good idea of what to expect."

"I can and will, Charlie. I have to swear you to secrecy though. The marketing plans are absolutely confidential."

Radar pulled out his folder to go over the marketing plans with Charlie. When Charlie left two hours later, his eyes were glazed. "This is worse than I expected," he thought.

6

Luke Shark was in a frenzy. His phone hadn't stopped ringing all morning. His first caller was Ferris Ferret, the business and labor columnist for *Happy Valley Sun News*.

"Mr. Shark, I understand you had quite a little altercation at the zoo yesterday."

"Oh, just a few of the boys getting a little carried away with a prank. Really, nothing to worry about, Ferris," Luke responded.

"That's not what I hear. Word has it there was extensive damage, and you didn't give the animals their pay. That's not good, Mr. Shark. First you lay off employees, and then you delay paychecks. What kind of an operation are you running? Are you having some kind of financial difficulty?"

"Ferris, I don't know where you got your information. I can assure you, I have been and will continue to be a fair and even-handed president. I certainly didn't withhold paychecks." Luke chuckled. "You know me better than that."

"I know you all right. And I wouldn't put anything past you."

Luke struggled to remain cordial.

"Now don't put me on like that, Ferris, you kidder. Everything is just fine here, and you are free to quote me."

"Don't worry, Luke. I will quote you, among others." Ferris hung up and the phone rang again.

"Luke Shark here."

"Good morning, Mr. Shark. My name is Bernard Owl, local commissioner of the Occupational Safety and Health Administration."

"What can I do for you?" Luke's mind worked fast.

"What the hell is going on here?" he wondered. "First Ferris, and now this Owl character."

"There have been some very disturbing accusations against you and the management of the zoo. Evidently conditions down there are extremely dangerous. I've been told you have a lot of construction with no barricades. My inspectors and I will be visiting you tomorrow. This call is your official notification."

"Commissioner, this is a mistake. Can't we talk about this a bit more? Tomorrow is Saturday, and I hadn't planned to be here."

"Suit yourself, Mr. Shark. I'll be there at nine o'clock in the morning." The phone went dead.

Luke looked out his window. There was construction everywhere. The zoo was a sea of mud. Construction vehicles were parked amid scattered piles of materials. It looked particularly bad after the riot. The inspectors would be able to find infractions, and plenty of them.

"What a goddamned mess!" he thought as he slammed down the phone.

Then another call came in.

"Luke Shark here."

"Mr. Shark, this is the American Society for the Prevention of Cruelty to Animals. We're had a serious complaint about your zoo's treatment of animals."

Luke was at the end of his rope.

"What the hell are you talking about, lady? We haven't been cruel to anyone. No one is less cruel to animals than this zoo."

"I hope you're right, Mr. Shark. Nevertheless, we will be sending a representative to inspect your zoo. I hope you will cooperate with this inspection. It will be much easier for you if you do."

"Send out your inspector. I don't give a damn. There's nothing to inspect."

"Very well, Mr. Shark. I had hoped you'd be more cooperative. We'll let you know the results." Once again the phone went dead. Luke had handled the call poorly.

"Damn!" he thought. "How much is a guy supposed to put up with in one day?"

He looked up to see Duane Beaver standing in his doorway.

"What is it, Beaver? Can't you see I'm busy?"

"The damage is terrible, Luke. I'm just sick about it. All that hard work for nothing. In a two-hour rampage they set us back almost three weeks, and I was behind schedule already." Duane waved his paws as he talked.

"You mean to tell me it's going to take you three weeks to clean up the mess?"

Duane jumped at the tone of Luke's voice.

"Well, I could finish it in two if the workers would just stop playing games. I can't get them to do anything anymore. I hardly have to look at them, and they have Muley on the scene. It's impossible for me to get anything done." Duane wiped his forehead, and his eyes darted about nervously.

"On top of that, my order of facing bricks didn't arrive. When I asked Jane about it, she just snapped at me and walked away. She's getting impossible, Luke."

"What do you want me to do about it, Duane? Tell Jane to quit picking on you?"

"No, I'm capable of handling my own affairs. Anyway, I just called the vendor directly, this morning. Know what he said? Someone from here cancelled the order. Right away I suspected Jane, but the guy said it was a male. I started screaming at the guy, asking him if he had a brain in his head. He got pretty hot himself and said he guessed if the acting president wanted to cancel an order he had a right."

Luke's head snapped up and he stared at Duane.

"What are you talking about?"

"That's what the guy said: 'If the acting president wanted to cancel an order, he had a right to do that.'"

"I didn't cancel your order. What a harebrained accusation."

"Well, someone cancelled it, and whoever it was said it was you."

"Did you tell the guy to ship the order?"

"Yes, but he said he'd have to hear it from you."

"It must be a plot to get rid of me, what else?" Luke thought. He could feel his heart racing and his breath was shallow. He realized Duane was still standing there.

"Is that all?"

"Will you call the guy?" Duane asked. He handed Luke a piece of paper with the vendor's name and number.

"This is an insult."

"It's the only way I'm going to get it, Luke."

"Okay, okay. I'll do it today. Now get out of here. I need to think."

• • •

The laid-off workers continued to report to the zoo every day, the mood lightening as they defined futures for themselves. Midway through the third week, representatives arrived from all eight divisions of Zoolandia International for a career fair: Theme Parks, Animal Food Products, Exotic Animal Ranches, Restaurants, Motel and Convention Centers, Zoolandia International Airlines, Zoolandia Management College, and

ZOO Radio and Television Broadcasting Network. Several local organizations also had booths. Each booth handed out small gifts, and before they were finished every animal had a sack of gifts and many had appointments for job interviews. Several Happy Valley employees tried to sneak into the career fair, but Charlie headed them off.

• • •

The BUZWA union reps agreed to visit two theme parks. Since the budget was limited, they sent four representatives—Amanda Chicken, Julia Peacock, Sam Penguin, and Arnold Antelope. As a gesture of good will, Mike Tiger arranged free passage on Zoolandia International Airlines (ZIA). They returned after a week and called an immediate rep meeting.

The four were full of interesting information about their visit. Amanda Chicken was most agitated. She had looked at the food operations; it was like nothing she had ever seen before. She talked about putting frozen meals into a cupboard, pushing buttons, and popping out a hot dinner. The other animals just looked at her in dumb silence.

"It's absolutely scary," Amanda said. "I don't know what kind of ingredients they have in that food. Who knows? And those cupboards they put them in look dangerous to me. If someone forgot to close the door, they could cook off a leg off before you said boo."

"Excuse me, folks. I've heard enough about magic for awhile. What you were supposed to find out was about ZAP and things like that," said Muley.

"We learned a lot about ZAP. From what I saw, they have a good contract, " Julia answered.

"I thought just the opposite." Sam looked at Julia. "I don't know where you're getting your information, Julia. Didn't you see the costumes they wore? And punching time clocks, too."

"Julia's right about the working rules. They're more liberal than ours. It's just that it's such a big operation it seems impersonal. I think ZAP can do more for us than BUZWA," Arnold chided Sam. "They have more experience with large organizations. BUZWA has concentrated on small zoos."

Everyone stopped and stared at Arnold.

"Are you out of your mind?" Sam demanded.

"No, he's not, Sam. I agree with him. ZAP can do more for us than BUZWA. I'm going to support ZAP in the election." Julia looked around the room to see if she and Arnold had any support.

"Don't look at me," brayed Muley. "I'm going for BUZWA."

The battle lines had been drawn.

Charlie got word of the disagreement among the reps and he was worried. Just when they needed to stick together, they were dividing into two camps. He talked to Julia.

"When is the election taking place?"

Julia looked at her datebook.

"Election day is October 25. The results will be announced on November 10."

"So we have two more weeks of campaign rhetoric. I'm worried that some of the wounds won't heal soon, Julia. Feelings run hot in union elections."

"I agree, Charlie. I'm very worried, too. I hope everyone uses their head."

Charlie and Julia agreed to stay in touch during the next two weeks. Charlie would keep his ears open and so would Julia. If they could head off trouble by working together, that's what they would do.

"Acquisitions can create the oddest alliances," Julia thought as she walked away.

• • •

Luke received a list of violations from the American Society for the Prevention of Cruelty to Animals. After that, the ASPCA had posted pickets outside the main gate. Its members were carrying signs: "Happy Valley management is imposing cruel and dangerous conditions on the animals." No amount of pleading or reasoning would get the picketers to leave until everything on the list was corrected, they said. Luke lost his temper. They better get used to walking in little circles outside the zoo because he had no intention of making all of those nitpicking changes, he said. He had stomped away and studiously ignored them ever since.

Ferris Ferret's article was worse than Luke expected. It included several pictures of the damage to the zoo. And as Ferris had promised, he quoted "unnamed highly placed sources" scathingly critical of Zoolandia and Luke. Someone sent a copy of the article to Mike Tiger, who called Luke that afternoon.

Luke had just received a notice of penalty from the Occupational Safety and Health Administration. He had four weeks to correct several infractions of animal safety regulations that OSHA had found. In addition, Happy Valley Zoo would have to pay a fine amounting to ten thousand dollars.

Duane had been back three times asking Luke to call vendors with news that their orders had not been cancelled. Luke would have thrown him out, but Duane was so agitated all he could do was agree. Duane's work was dangerously behind schedule. Still, Zoolandia had plans to open the new buildings before the holidays.

Mike Tiger arrived the next day.

"Close your door, Luke, we have some serious things to discuss."

"What's up, Mike? You sound official."

"There are several things of great concern to us, Luke. First of all, it looks like no one is in charge here. You've had a string of mishaps that most presidents don't encounter in a lifetime. I don't know how much of it is bad luck and how much incompetence, but you've got to get a handle on this operation."

When Luke started to speak, Mike cut him off.

"I don't need excuses, Luke. Just let my statement stand as a warning. Now, there are a few things that need to get done. Happy Valley is a bigger cash drain than we expected. Your revenue doesn't justify your expenditures, and you've got to make a 10-percent budget cut, effective immediately. I don't care how you do it. Just get it done."

"How can we possibly cut now? We're struggling just to stay alive."

"You're losing money, and your purse strings have just been tightened, period." Mike sat quietly for awhile, his silence challenging.

Luke waited him out. He was learning.

"Another thing that's a mess is the construction schedule," Mike continued. "Zoolandia has scheduled an opening for the theme park, and we're not changing it to accommodate Beaver's schedule. I've instructed Ted Tiger to send in Zoolandia construction crews to finish the job. Ted will personally oversee the construction, and Duane will report to him. The construction workers will be living in trailers arriving before the end of the week. Ted has looked over the area. The only logical place to put the trailers is behind the Watering Hole."

"You're asking for another riot. The union is not going to want someone else here doing their job. On top of that, the Zoolandia workers will be staying all around the Watering Hole. My God, what a powder keg."

"I was wondering about that myself. We'll just have to close down the Watering Hole until construction is complete. The last thing I'm going to tell you requires no action from you, Luke. I'm telling you because as acting president you've a right to know. We have two security guards here now, and we've taken Willy Weasel in for questioning. They have him in a conference room. We'll keep him there until we get some answers."

"What are you asking him about? He just runs the souvenir shop."

"He's been sabotaging the zoo, Luke. If you had kept your eyes and ears open, you'd have figured it out yourself. Why do you think you've been hearing from all these agencies? Did you check his long-distance log? And didn't you wonder who was canceling all the orders with vendors?"

Luke felt stupid.

"Of course, who else but Willy?" he thought. "Why didn't I think of that?"

"What are you going to do with him, Mike?"

"It depends on what we find out. He's made some serious accusations, some of which may be true. We need to check them out. The only thing we haven't decided is whether we'll just fire him or fire him and press charges for sabotage and unauthorized use of company resources. I'll let you know. In any case, we'll escort him off the property as soon as we're done questioning him. He's not to be on the zoo property again. We'll see to it he doesn't forget."

"Zoolandia doesn't play around," Luke thought.

He was right. At that moment Willy was locked in a room with two of the meanest-looking dogs he'd ever seen. At first he denied everything, next tried bribing his questioners, and finally he began to talk.

Willy had been the one to call the agencies and the local newspaper. The calls to Atlantic City were to see whether Shark was a member of the mob. He hadn't been able to find out. Willy admitted he had no knowledge of anything out of the way about Roy's death and Hamilton's breakdown, and the dogs made him sign a statement to that effect. Then they pulled him to his feet and marched him out the door to the front gate. One dog told him he wouldn't be safe if he tried to enter any Zoolandia property again.

• • •

Luke closed the door when Mike left. This job of acting president was a nightmare. A 10-percent budget cut was no small thing. He sat so still no one would have known he wasn't sleeping but for the occasional expletive.

Finally Mike pulled out a pad and started jotting down figures. He wasn't fooled. He knew the only way he could make such a cut was to have another layoff. This time he would make the decisions himself and give his staff their quotas. He'd had enough bickering. He rang for Wendy.

"Yes, Luke? Did you need something?"

"No. I rang for the hell of it," he snapped. "Get me the organization charts."

Wendy returned and handed them to Luke.

"These have been updated since the layoff, Luke."

"Good. That helps."

Wendy left, closing the door behind her. Luke poured over the charts. The last cut had been painful for salaried employees. Some departments could barely cover their work. This time it would have to be union workers. Fifty workers should do it. He started with Carl Crocodile's operations chart.

"Tram conductors are obsolete. They can hardly get through the construction site now. We'll just shut down the operation." He jotted down all twenty penguins for layoff. "That means no tram maintenance. Duane can take a 10-percent cut in maintenance monkeys."

He jotted down the names of ten monkeys.

"Duane's going to get all this help from Zoolandia, so I'll make a few cuts there," and he listed five mules and rhinos from Construction and Move Crew, eight bears from Janitorial, and four antelopes from Groundskeeping. Luke added up the numbers. He needed three more.

"I've got it, we'll just cut Ms. Peacock's production staff in half."

He wrote three peacock names. Luke sat back in his chair and scanned the list. He calculated again.

"Fifty workers should make the budget cut. Better get this rolling right away."

He buzzed Wendy for dictation. A few minutes later she was typing a memo to Luke's staff announcing the layoffs. She shook her head.

"Will this never end?" she thought as she delivered the memo.

When Duane arrived, Shark was prepared for him.

"Shut the door, Beaver. We have more to talk about than the layoff, which I'm sure is why you're here."

"You're damned right that's why I'm here! You must be crazy, telling me to lay off all those workers. Haven't you been listening? I'm falling further and further behind. I can't afford to lose a single worker. As a matter of fact, I could use double what I have."

"Don't worry, Beaver. That's exactly what you're getting."

"What are you talking about?"

"Apparently Zoolandia doesn't think you're capable of running the construction competently. They're bringing in their own construction crews. Ted Tiger will be in charge, and you'll be reporting to him. With the extra help, you won't need those workers on the layoff list."

Duane stared.

"I don't believe this. It's just impossible. Has the whole world gone crazy? I've been working myself half to death, and all I get are problems and criticism. Well, let Tiger try his hand. He'll soon find out it's impossible. No one can accomplish what they expect. Let them do what they want. I've had it. I really have."

He was still ranting as he slammed the door.

News of the layoff dramatically heated debate between ZAP and BUZWA. On the heels of the news came the Zoolandia construction crews. Trailer after trailer was towed in and parked around the Watering Hole. Flatbed trucks with sophisticated construction equipment followed. Luke walked down and posted a notice on the door of the Watering Hole: "Closed until further notice." He had the security department put a padlock on the door, then stomped back to his office.

Charlie watched the construction equipment arrive. He had known about the crews, but seeing them arrive was a shock.

"Charlie, got a minute?" Radar Dolphin stood in the doorway.

"Sure Radar. I was just watching the new arrivals. I'm worried about how this is going to affect our workers. They can't take much more pushing around."

"I agree. That's why I'm here. How 'bout if you and I make a point of walking around and talking to workers. Maybe we can prevent a nasty reaction."

"That's a great idea for you, Radar, but I'm the company man—the adversary."

"I suppose you're right. Still, I'm going to do what I can. Damn that Luke. Things would have been so much better if he'd called an employee meeting and talked to them about this. They have to learn everything through the rumor mill or by nasty surprise."

Radar was about to leave when Julia, Grinder, Muley, Arnold, and Sweeper burst into Charlie's office.

"What's the meaning of all of this, Fox? First you lay off people. Then you replace them with Zoolandia workers," demanded Grinder Monkey. "You've asked for it this time. It's all-out war."

"Hold on, Grinder. Things are bad enough without you getting crazy."

"Keep out of this, Radar. It's not your fight."

"The hell it isn't! This is my zoo, too, and anyone who wants to destroy it is part of my business. Now listen, all of you. This is a hell of a thing that's happening. No one realizes it more than me. But you can't fight it with violence. Zoolandia is bigger and stronger than all you workers put together. It's like throwing yourself against a brick wall."

"What are you suggesting, Radar?"

"The first thing I'm suggesting is that you reps get out there and calm down your workers. There's nothing good going to come from violence. Then call a meeting of the reps and put together a strategy."

"That's all fine and dandy, Radar, but we just lost our meeting room. The Watering Hole has been closed down." Grinder hardly concealed his rage.

"Come on, Grinder. You can find a place to meet."

Charlie suddenly came to life.

"I've got it. How about using the company picnic tent? It will hold enough tables and chairs for meetings, and if the weather's bad, you can drop the sides."

"Just where would you suggest we pitch it, Charlie? The place is a sea of mud."

"I know a place," said Arnold, the groundskeeper. "There's a level area outside the back gate that is covered with grass. The gate has electricity, and we can plug into it if we need anything."

"What if we turned it into the temporary Watering Hole?" Julia asked.

Charlie thought for a minute.

"That's possible. You workers need a place to meet and that's that. I don't want you going through the Zoolandia trailers either. It's asking for trouble. No, that's it. I'll get the tent out of storage this afternoon. If you animals can move the equipment out of the Watering Hole without altercations, I think we're in business."

"Now, as I was saying," Radar reminded them, "you reps need to get out there and get the workers calmed down. I'll do the same thing myself." As he finished, they heard the buses of construction workers arrive.

Julia took charge.

"Let's get word to the workers there'll be a union meeting at the new Watering Hole at 7:00 P.M. Tell everyone not to take action on their own. We need to fight this together."

"I say let's go out there and start bashing heads." Grinder was looking out the window at the buses.

Charlie stepped in front of him.

"Violence isn't the answer. You've got better weapons."

"Oh, is that so?" Grinder's sarcasm was exaggerated. "What weapons do we have, Mr. Labor Relations?"

"Think about it a minute. There are other unionized workers besides BUZWA."

"What the hell does that have to do with anything?" Grinder began.

Julia cut him off.

"Charlie, my boy, sometimes you amaze me. Come on, Grinder. Let's get moving. We have to get the Watering Hole set up and plan for the meeting. And let's get out there and spread the word." Julia looked back at Charlie.

"Amazing," she muttered, "simply amazing."

At seven o'clock, the new Watering Hole was jammed with animals. Those who couldn't get in, squeezed around the edges of the tent. The flaps were raised so everyone could see the stage and the speakers. It was a cold evening, and the animals moved restlessly about. The BUZWA reps took seats on the stage and talked animatedly among themselves.

Sam Penguin rose and picked up the portable microphone used at the annual company picnic. At first, his voice could not penetrate the din. But little by little, the animals began to pay attention.

"Ladies and gentlemen," Sam began in the elegant manner he usually reserved for his monologue on the tram. "I'm pleased you all could come tonight."

"Get on with it, Penguin." The animals were in no mood for pleasantries.

"Yes, yes—of course," Sam cleared his throat and began again. "We have important things to discuss here. As you no doubt noticed, there are Zoolandia construction crews residing on our property."

"Are you going to get on with it or am I going to have to come up there myself?" a loud voice boomed.

Julia stood, and Sam gratefully turned the microphone over to her.

"That's exactly what we're going to do. We've called this meeting because we're in the fight of our lives, and it's important we do it right. Zoolandia has violated our contract by bringing in construction crews. We intend to protect that contract. We've put a plan together that will work if everyone cooperates and sticks with the plan. Since it's the construction workers' contract, Muley will outline our strategy."

Muley wasted no time. A picket line would be set up early the next morning. The Zoolandia construction workers were members of ZAP, and they would have to decide whether or not to cross a union picket line. There would be pickets at the front gate and at the service gate. The delivery truck drivers were all unionized and wouldn't cross. The union could effectively shut down the zoo—without violence.

As Muley finished outlining the plan, the animals were quiet enough to hear a pin drop, an uneasy moment for the reps. But little by little the animals began to talk to each other, and soon their discussions became a roar. Laughter swirled about and smiles appeared on the animals' faces. The animals milled around, slapped each other on the back, and shouted encouragement. They were more animated than they had been in weeks.

The next morning, Luke was confronted by a picket line at the front gate. He recognized several of Muley's workers walking back and forth with signs: "Union Busting." Luke rolled down the car window to yell at the workers when he was blinded by a flash.

"Smile, Mr. Shark. Your picture will be on the front page this evening, " said Ferris Ferret, the business and labor columnist for *Happy Valley Sun News.*

Luke rolled up his window and drove through the gate. He didn't stop until he had reached his office and closed the door. From his office window, he assessed the situation. A line of delivery trucks was parked outside the service gate, the drivers standing in a clump around the mules. Luke watched the drivers return to their trucks and drive off.

"They're not making their deliveries!" Luke shouted to the window. "What the hell is going on?"

Just then he looked at the construction site, surrounded by more than fifty picketers carrying signs like the ones at the front gate. Motion off to the side caught Luke's attention. The Zoolandia construction workers were coming from their living quarters. Luke held his breath.

"Oh my God, not another riot," he groaned. He couldn't take his eyes off the scene playing before his office window. As the construction workers neared the picketers, they walked more and slowly, as if they weren't sure what they should do. Luke saw Julia Peacock step out of line and walk up to them. Engulfed by larger animals, she disappeared. Luke saw her again as the construction workers turned back to their living quarters.

"Those S.O.B.'s are going back!" Luke practically exploded. "What the hell am I going to do now?"

He fell back into his chair when the phone jolted him.

"Yes, what is it?" Luke forgot to announce his title.

"Luke, what the hell's going on down there?" said Mike Tiger. "I heard something on the national news this morning about union busting at Happy Valley Zoo."

"I don't know, Mike. I just got here. I haven't figured it out. There are animals carrying signs and truck drivers leaving and I don't know what." Luke's voice trailed off.

"I'm catching the ten o'clock, and I'll be there by noon. Don't do anything until I get there. Try to keep things from erupting."

"Erupting? Erupting?" Luke rambled as he slammed down the phone. "That's what every day is around here, one big eruption! And you want me to keep things from erupting?"

Mike, too, was greeted by marchers at the front gate. Instead of going on through, he got out of the car to talk with the picketers.

"Sorry, we don't talk to management. Our representatives are at the command post," they said, still walking back and forth.

Mike went directly to Luke's office. Small and frail, Wendy was sitting at her desk. Mike saw the inner strength that had sustained her through all these years. A coldly polite good morning and a turned back replaced the welcome he usually enjoyed.

Luke was still sitting in his chair, staring out the window.

"What's happened since we talked?" Mike started.

"Nothing. Just animals walking around carrying signs. No deliveries, no construction, no customers, no nothing." Luke was rambling uncharacteristically.

"Where's Fox? Has he been talking with the union?"

"I saw him running around out there a while ago. I think he may have been at the Watering Hole."

"Where is he now?" Mike's voice commanded. "Never mind, I'll find him myself."

He picked up his briefcase and closed the door on his way out.

Charlie was sitting in his office with his contract book open when Mike walked in.

"What the hell's going on, Fox?"

"One big mess, I'd say. The employees are picketing the construction site, and they've managed to shut down the zoo."

"What's the matter with those idiots? Are they trying to destroy this place? Don't they know their jobs are on the line?"

"They have never been clearer about their jobs being on the line, Mike," Charlie began. "That's what the picketing is all about. You've just violated several major portions of their contract by bringing in Zoolandia construction crews. And your timing stinks. Remember, we just laid off construction workers."

Mike looked at Charlie. He was about to snap back, but something about Charlie made him reconsider.

"What do you recommend we do? We can't afford bad publicity."

Charlie frowned.

"I don't give a damn about publicity. I'm concerned about the workers and maintaining the integrity of the contracts. If Larry Lion did his job right, this mess would never have happened."

Mike nodded for Charlie to continue.

"First of all, you've got to recall the laid-off construction and move crews. There are five altogether. Next, you've got to negotiate with the union for a one-time, nonprecedent agreement to complete construction. They're not going to give it to you without concessions."

"What kind of concessions?" Mike listened intently.

"I asked them the same thing this morning. The construction workers want time-and-a-half pay during the time the Zoolandia construction crews are here, and they want to take their vacations at the same time." Charlie held up a paw as Mike opened his mouth.

"Wait, wait. Hear me out. Beaver canceled their vacations because construction was behind schedule. They've always taken their vacation at the end of the summer season, and they all have vacation coming."

"What else?" Mike snapped

"They want direct access to you. They're not interested in any more nasty surprises."

"I can't have that."

"They want to designate one rep as their liaison with you. I think you'd better agree. They've got you in a tight spot, and they know it," Charlie said.

"All right. I'll agree to that but nothing more."

"Just one more thing." Charlie continued. "They want you to come to their command post personally and talk with them."

"You get them to pull their pickets, and I'll meet them at the command post."

"Can I tell them you agree to the terms? Otherwise they won't pull the pickets."

"Work out the agreement, Charlie, and let me know when they're ready for me to come. I want to talk to all the union workers, not just the reps."

It was late afternoon when the union gathered to hear what Mike Tiger had to say. As he stood on the stage, looking out at the crowd, he knew he was facing a strong adversary. They had taken on an international conglomerate and they had won.

"With the back-to-work agreement we signed today, we have made the first major step in working together as part of the same team. I want to apologize to each of you for the misunderstandings that have occurred this week. I welcome your idea of a union liaison who will stay in touch with me to avoid another incident. I also want to reassure you there will be no retribution for picketing, and the visiting construction crews will not displace any Happy Valley workers."

There was a long silence when Mike finished. No one applauded. Instead the workers turned to one another and began slapping paws, congratulating one another. This was their celebration, and Mike was not a part of it. He quietly left the tent for his car.

• • •

Once the strike was over, the animals turned their attention of to the union elections. Sweeper and his bears rented a hot air balloon and flew it over the zoo, dropping hundreds of BUZWA leaflets. They particularly peppered the construction trailers, but the leaflets stuck in the mud, where no one could read them. Arnold's crew was sent out to clean up the mess.

On the second day the Zoolandia construction crews were at work, a terrorized Big Al Boa turned himself in to Morley Mongoose. He had been hiding in the tall grass near the old picnic area for weeks, barely escaping an earth mover.

"A guy could get killed out there," he told Morley as he climbed into a cage for his trip to the Zoolandia Exotic Animal Farm.

The zoo was quickly transformed into a theme park. Buildings took shape. New walks and roadways were paved. The Happy Valley animals had never seen so much concrete, and they began to worry there wouldn't be any grass at all. Three large artificial ponds were surrounded by benches and tables. Next came truckload after truckload of trees and shrubs for planting on the contoured areas. The mud disappeared as it was replaced by foliage and buildings.

Workers turned in their sealed ballots for the union election and returned to work. There was nothing to do but wait. Both sides were claiming victory, but it was too close to call.

7

Relief spread across the zoo. Construction was complete, the laid-off animals were gone, and it looked as if like things would settle down during the slow winter season. The union election was tabulated. The announcement that ZAP had won was almost anticlimactic. Most of the animals put that struggle behind. Campaign posters came down. ZAP held victory meetings, then began to prepare for negotiating transition agreements.

Charlie and Radar had arranged for all employees to have a tour of the new buildings. They were awed by the sleek, modern interiors. At the end of each tour, the animals were escorted into the new convention center meeting hall. Charlie and Radar talked about the future of Happy Valley Theme Park. They talked about more changes coming, new procedures and new kinds of events. The animals would be expected to learn a new way of doing business. The animals listened but didn't worry. That was a long way off. They would have the winter to rest. They were just going to enjoy the holidays and sleep, sleep, sleep.

But the tranquility was short-lived. Mike Tiger arrived at the zoo, setting a whirlwind into motion. Suddenly Luke Shark was gone, and Mike Tiger had replaced him. An organization announcement followed. Then changes filtered down to the lower levels. The Zoolandia automated system replaced Maynard Skunk's payroll department. Maynard and his workers were moved into accounts payable and receivable. Jane Porcupine resumed her old position as supervisor of the souvenir shop. Her workers moved to the phone order section of marketing. Corporate headquarters would handle all purchasing.

Charlie had permission to hire a new labor relations lawyer, and he had been advertising in the zoo professional journals. Sarah had two openings—one for manager of planning, the other for controller.

Zoolandia International

Memorandum
November 11

To: Zoolandia Employees
Theme Park 46
From: Mike Tiger
President
Dept: Theme Park 46
Zoolandia Theme Park Division
Subject: Organization Announcement

Effective immediately, Zoolandia Theme Park Number 46 is a self-contained organizational unit maintaining profit-center status. All operations and support management personnel report to the president, whose staff includes:

- Vice President, Finance and Administration, Sarah B. Giraffe. Sarah has been acting in this capacity and will assume responsibilities full time. She brings to this position several years of experience in strategic planning as well as in-depth understanding of data processing and the Zoolandia financial systems.

- Vice President, Operations, Carl Crocodile. Carl continues in his critical operations role with renewed emphasis on quality service and responsiveness to Zoolandia customers in the many programs being instituted over the next twelve months.

- Vice President, Personnel and Labor Relations, Charles Fox. Charlie has been Labor Relations Manager for a number of years and, over the past few months, assumed responsibility for personnel as well. He has been formally promoted and will continue to manage both functions. He will act

(continued)

> (Organization announcement, continued)
>
>   as liaison with Zoolandia in matters of corporate personnel policy.
>
> • Vice President, Marketing, Radar Dolphin. Radar will continue his position with special emphasis on new promotion and the special events program.
>
> • Vice President, Maintenance, William Bennett Woodchuck. Will joins us from Zoolandia Theme Park Number 71 where he has been Director of Roads and Parklands since 1963. He brings a wealth of experience in the areas of woodlands management and exhibit revitalization.
>
> Please join me in wishing the staff continued success in their challenging assignments. All staff will subscribe to the Zoolandia open door policy and management by walking around. Feel free to congratulate workers personally and offer your support. I appreciate your cooperation.

Duane Beaver's name was noticeably off the list. He had accepted a maintenance position at the municipal zoo in Tumwater, Iowa.

Julia Peacock arrived promptly at one o'clock for her appointment with Mike Tiger. She was surprised to see drastic changes in Colonel's old office. Gone were the heavy, old mahogany pieces. They were replaced by blond oak furniture with clean, angular lines. On one side table was a computer terminal, its screen on, its cursor blinking. Muted watercolors lined the wall. There wasn't a certificate in sight.

"Come in, Julia." Mike got up, offering Julia a seat at the round table placed in a corner of the room.

"I can't get over how different Colonel's office looks," Julia said.

"No more different than the changes around the theme park. Well, what do you think? Is it a change for the better?"

"The changes to the office are a definite improvement. The ones to Happy Valley Zoo—well, the jury is still out."

"You don't mince words. I like your directness. As a matter of fact, that's why I've asked you here. I have the pleasure of offering you a position in Theatrical Productions." Mike paused for emphasis.

"A management position. What do you think? "

"I'm flattered and pleased," Julia responded. "But I've already accepted a position with ZAP."

"Why would a talented bird like you get mixed up with the unions? You'd have a much brighter future with a forward-thinking corporation like Zoolandia."

"I'm not surprised at your response, Mr. Tiger. Don't think I'm not aware of the excellent opportunity you offer. A few years ago I would have grabbed it. My creative talents haven't exactly been stretched here at Happy Valley."

"Then why not take it?" Mike couldn't resist interrupting.

"I'm about to tell you why. Something else has become much more important to me lately—the animals. They have no one but the union to represent their interests. I've discovered I have a talent and—don't laugh—a passion for it."

"I won't laugh, Julia. I don't think there's anything wrong with passion for a job."

"It's more than a job to me. I've seen what mismanagement of employees can do. For example, you've miscalculated the employees here at Happy Valley from the very beginning. I still don't think you understand the culture. We've all been like one big family, with Colonel the father. He was accessible and he cared about every one of us—unlike the mystical Zoolandia that hands down edicts from afar.

"You want to know one of the crueler moves you've made? The way you gagged Colonel and then shunted him off in the dark of night. No farewell, nothing. Did you know Luke Shark threw Colonel out of this very office?"

Mike stood up and started for the door.

"I'm convinced, Julia. You don't want the job."

"Please hear me out."

Mike stopped with his paw on the door knob and turned.

"I'm not interested in any more lectures about Zoolandia's screw-ups—or mine."

"I'm trying to show you where the mistakes happened so we can avoid them in the future. You and I are going to be working the same issues from opposite sides of the table. Seems to me it would be better for both of us if we can talk things over."

"Are you turning this into an official union visit?"

"No, nothing official. I just wanted to assure you that I want to work with you not, against you. In the best interests of us both." Julia rose and started for the door as Mike opened it.

"Thanks for the offer and for your time." The door closed softly behind her.

• • •

The animals began seeing ads in the local newspaper for weekend packages at Zoolandia Theme Park 46. The next series of ads was for holiday parties at the zoo. Suddenly it began to dawn on them—there was going to be much more activity than usual during the winter.

Sheldon Seal was back from Zoolandia headquarters with a new menu of classes and workshops to offer. He had been promoted to di-

---

HAPPY VALLEY SUN TIMES

Zoolandia Offers Abba Dabba Honeymoon

By Harry Zumwalt
Staff Writer

Have you even considered a wild animal wedding with a honeymoon to match, or brunch with a bear, or a formal tea with tigers? Zoolandia Theme Park offers all these options and many more to the patron with a bit of imagination and willingness to pay for it.

Zoolandia representatives announced today that the theme park and all animals will be available to create a unique and personal backdrop for any occasion. "The event may be large or intimate, simple or complex. We can handle it," stated Radar Dolphin of the Zoolandia marketing office.

"We have available a complete line of catering, a decorating staff, event planners, and serving personnel, as well as a cooperative and entertaining staff of animals. Add that to this lovely setting and our new flexible facilities for a unique and memorable experience for you and your guests."

Other Zoolandia theme parks have hosted a wide range of events including weddings, birthday parties and christenings, anniversaries, civic affairs, intimate dinners for two, proms, business meetings and in 1976, the Republican National Convention.

Fourteen events have already been scheduled for the next month as the holiday season approaches.

rector of Training and Development, and three trainers—Sam Penguin and two of his former tram conductors—now worked for him full time.

Sheldon and his trainers brought in entire departments for training in procedures radically different from anything they had experienced before. Each job category was issued a costume, to be worn at all times on the job.

The holidays were getting closer, and the animals were involved in learning about their new world. The week before Thanksgiving the floodgates opened, and thousands of customers descended on Theme Park 46. The hotel and convention center were jammed to overflowing. What had been practice for the animals during training was multiplied by a thousand for the real thing.

Amanda and her chickens worked in the restaurant in white lace aprons and perky matching hats. A sleek, smooth-talking rooster from Zoolandia had trained them to prepare food according to Zoolandia specifications. They ran around the convention center kitchen, clucking and pecking, their aprons long since wilted, their hats lost. They staggered taking the heavy trays to the dining room. The squirrels in the dishwashing room were drenched with sweat. One squirrel caught his tail in the conveyer belt and lost a patch of fur. He had a towel tied around his wound as he struggled with the never-ending stream of dirty dishes. Shattering plates punctuated the din.

Chef Rodney Rooster was everywhere at once. He watched in dismay as his ten-day inventory disappeared on the second day. He put in an emergency call to headquarters, asking for an order by air express.

Jane Porcupine and her souvenir-shop workers wore long grass skirts with flower leis. The souvenir shop was a madhouse. Sales of Zoolandia products were brisk, and shelves had to be constantly restocked. The grass skirts flashed as the clerks tried to keep up with customer demand. All signs of Happy Valley were gone from the souvenir shop. No more stuffed elephants or miniature trams.

Sweeper and his maintenance engineers, dressed in orange jumpsuits, careened among the guests in three-wheel carts painted like orange street sweepers, trying to keep up with the clutter.

All the exhibit animals were under great stress. They had to be at their exhibits an hour before the park opened to spruce things up, shine their coats, and put on their "subtle, not flashy" make-up. No more just sitting and watching customers walk by. Roaring animals were to roar, and cute animals were to act cute. The exhibit area was a stage, and the animals were to "act" at all times. The bears took turns sneaking into the cave for a reprieve from standing on their back legs and growling.

The monkeys got muscle spasms from their constant swinging through the branches. Their exhibit started to have the odor of Ben Gay®.

Theatrical Productions was in total disarray without Julia Peacock. The three remaining peacocks put on two performances a day—not the performing bird shows of the past. All exhibit animals were expected to perform on a regular schedule in addition to carrying out their exhibit duties. The peacocks designed and produced costumes for all categories of exhibit animals, choreographed the shows, and trained the animals. It was an impossible task. Most animals didn't have a shred of talent or interest. They went through the motions mechanically, and no amount of prodding helped.

The animals in the marketing department didn't fare any better. Reservation lines were jammed. By the time customers got through, they were irritated and rude to the clerks. Zoolandia had a package plan for almost any contingency—weekends, full weeks, overnight, full-meal plans, rooms with a ticket packet for theme park rides and mid-way attractions, and rooms only. There were packages with or without travel on Zoolandia International Airlines (ZIA). The formulas for figuring rates were complicated. Each clerk sat at a computer terminal, wearing a telephone headset. As each call was disconnected, another automatically came through. There was no time to take a breath between calls, and no matter how fast the the animals worked, the line-up of calls never diminished. The overloaded computer system crashed several times a day. Orders taken manually when the system was down created double booking errors.

At the hotel, the penguins worked the front desk in their red bow ties and black top hats. The hotel was overbooked every night, and the penguins spent most of their time trying to secure alternate lodgings for customers. The bellhops, former maintenance and ground crew employees, routinely delivered the wrong luggage to the wrong rooms, occasionally mixing up the luggage of those coming with those going. One convention center elevator broke when a mule hit two buttons at once. The elevator expert from Zoolandia didn't arrive for two days. There was a continuous jam waiting to go up or down the remaining three elevators.

• • •

Charlie watched the chaos and worried. And when there was a brief lull a few days after Thanksgiving, he went to see Mike Tiger.

"Mike, I'm concerned with what I'm seeing. The animals are trying harder than they ever have, and it's just not enough. We're staffed too thin."

"I agree the employees are working harder than ever, but don't forget this is all new to them. As they become more comfortable with their responsibilities, things will ease up."

"Come on, Mike. You can't believe we have enough employees to handle this volume on a sustained basis."

"Happy Valley had been losing money for a long time. Those layoffs were necessary to bring costs in line with profits. The issue is revenue. It isn't up yet."

"And never will be if you don't allow some hiring. The animals will drop like flies. They've about reached the end of their endurance."

"I'm sorry, Charlie. We can't hire until the new year."

"We'll never make it through Christmas, Mike."

"We'll have to. That's all there is to it."

"If the budget for next year will allow hiring, I want to spend the month of December recruiting, so we'll have employees ready to start work on January 2."

"Do you have numbers?"

"I have ballpark figures in mind. The best plan would be to have your staff make headcount plans for the next year. Then we can put together a hiring schedule."

"Get right on it, and tell my staff to have their figures ready for the next regular staff meeting. I don't just want numbers, though. They'll have to justify every hire against the bottom line."

Charlie had no sooner left Mike's office than Mike received a call from Elliott Elephant, president of the Theme Park Division. Elliott checked with Mike regularly.

"How are the animals reacting to all the changes, Mike?"

"Better than I expected."

"Good, glad to hear it. Keep up the good work, Mike. You'll never have more visibility at Zoolandia than you do now."

• • •

Every employee at TP-46 was strained to the limit meeting job demands during December. Mike put out a memo to all supervisory personnel saying that they were to work at least forty-eight hours per week until the first of the year. Unnecessary administrative functions were to be postponed, and whenever possible, assistance was to be given to areas unable to meet the demand. All vacation was canceled, all training suspended.

Customer complaints soared, and the customer relations department begged for help. Mike Tiger instructed his staff to spend one day a week helping to handle customer complaints.

Through December, Charlie recruited new employees. Mike's staff had come up with a hiring plan for the next year. Twenty of the employees laid off in summer were available for rehire and set to start on January 2. Recalled union workers would also start January 2 along with a hundred new employees. Charlie extended an offer to a bright young labor relations lawyer. He was waiting to see whether she would accept.

Arnold Antelope's groundskeepers worked at a frenzied pace to decorate the park for Christmas. They hung hundreds of strings of lights along the walkways, installed four extensive nativity scenes, and decorated forty Christmas trees including a twenty-foot blue spruce on the convention center lawn. TP-46 was transformed into a winter fairyland.

For the first time in their lives, the animals had to work on Christmas. Sheldon Seal dressed as Santa Claus. He stationed himself in the main lobby, greeting customers and giving children gaily wrapped gifts. The theatrical productions group put on a Christmas pageant, and the Bird's Singing Choir sang carols. When the day was over, the tired animals went home to their families to begin their own celebrations.

• • •

The new year finally arrived, and everyone breathed a sign of relief. They had survived barely, but they had survived. But when the pace didn't slow, the workers realized it wasn't going to be just a stressful holiday season. It would be that way all year round.

New workers arrived to lighten the load. But they needed training and it would be weeks before they were productive. In the meantime, the old employees continued under the strain of a crushing workload.

One morning, early in April, Charlie Fox went to Mike's office.

"I was thinking it's time to have an employee celebration."

"What's to celebrate, Charlie? The employees are not yet efficient, and the union contract still hasn't been signed."

"Think about it, Mike. There's a helluva lot to celebrate. Look what the animals have accomplished in the past few months. They've pulled off miracles."

Mike sat quietly and listened.

"If they can see what they've done and they're recognized for it, they may be able to get through the next few months a bit easier."

"You're right, Charlie. It's a good idea. If we can give them the spirit to make it through the next few months, why not? Maybe I could talk to them and show them there is a light at the end of the tunnel."

"I don't think they know there is an ongoing hiring plan."

"They're getting more efficient. I can see the improvements in the numbers every week," Mike added. "Zoolandia has a standard employee celebration package we can use. You and Radar will be in charge of arrangements."

On a Monday evening in May, the park closed three hours early, and the celebration began with a catered dinner in the convention center. All supervisory and management staff worked while employees were guests of the park. At each place setting was a small gift—a pen-and-pencil set with the Zoolandia logo. An engraved card with each set, reading "In appreciation for outstanding performance," was personally signed by Mike Tiger.

Mike gave a short speech congratulating and thanking the animals. He told them of his first impression when he visited Happy Valley Zoo, and how he wondered if they would be able to transform it into a theme park. He described how he began to have more and more respect for the animals as he watched them continue to perform under difficult conditions. And he assured them help was on the way. A procession of new employees and equipment was arriving daily. The worst was over.

"Look around this theme park and be proud. It's your theme park as much as Zoolandia's. Your signatures are all over it, and without all of you this never would have happened. Happy Valley is gone forever, and in its place you have built the most modern theme park in the world. Give yourself a hand, TP-46, you deserve it," Mike finished his speech. He started clapping. The room went wild, and the younger animals leapt to their feet, cheering. They began hugging each other and slapping each other on the back, laughing and crying. Yes, they had come a long way, and no one could be prouder.

The older workers were less enthusiastic. They still longed for the Happy Valley days and would keep the old traditions alive where they could. But they knew they would conform to Zoolandia's ways in order to survive. Still, they were proud of their ability to adapt and survive.

The animals were reluctant to end the good feeling by leaving the convention hall. Finally they began to filter out to the park where their families joined them for rides on the monorail, games on the midway, and a theatrical production brought in especially from ZOO Broadcasting Network. The kids got balloons and all the snacks they could eat.

The next day the animals could hardly talk about anything else. They said it was the most fun they ever had, and now they understood why customers loved to visit the theme park. Morale soared. But the work was relentless, and the animals quickly came back to reality.

• • •

Along with the new employees came a visitor from the past when Colonel, the former president of Happy Valley Zoo, visited TP-46. His job as Zoolandia lobbyist in Washington, D.C., had not lasted as long as he expected, greatly disappointing him. Colonel hadn't told anyone he was coming—he thought he'd make it a surprise. And he wasn't prepared for what he saw. Coming through the front gate, he saw not a trace of the old Happy Valley Zoo. He was quickly lost without the familiar landmarks. The workers, all in costume, looked like strangers. Finally he saw someone he recognized.

"Hello there, Sam," he shouted.

Sam Penguin turned around and looked. It was a minute before he recognized Colonel.

"Colonel, it's nice to see you. What brings you back here?"

"Oh, just wanted to see how everyone was doing. This is quite a place. Where is the tram? You still work on the tram, don't you?"

"Oh no, I haven't done that in ages. Theme parks don't have trams, don't you know? We have a monorail system. You should ride it."

"Of course, of course," Colonel said. "What are you doing, Sam, if the tram is gone?"

"I'm working for Sheldon in the training department. Who would have thought I'd end up in a job like that?" Sam looked at his watch. "I've got to run. I have a training session starting in five minutes, and we're strict about starting on time. Good seeing you again, Colonel. Stop by again when I have time to talk."

As Sam rushed toward the training facility, two young workers stopped him.

"Hey, Sam, who is that old elephant? He's been wandering around here like he's lost."

"Oh, that's Colonel. He used to be president here."

"Really, when was that?"

"It seems like ages and ages ago."

• • •

On a Saturday night in June, Mike scheduled an appreciation dinner to recognize management's hard work. It was held in a private dining room at the motel and convention center; an engraved silver plaque with the Zoolandia logo graced each place setting. Below the logo was engraved the manager's name followed by "In appreciation for outstanding performance."

Mike was to sit at the head table with his staff members. They became concerned when Mike didn't arrive at the beginning of the dinner.

"This isn't like Mike to be late."

Sarah looked around the room at the round tables filled with animals dressed in their finest.

"Something must have delayed him, Sarah. He'll be right along."

Charlie was feeling particularly fine tonight. His new labor relations attorney had started work that week and had already been set up a get-acquainted appointment with Julia. Charlie was relieved to be turning over that responsibility to her.

He looked Sarah, who was chatting with Carl Crocodile. She appeared more relaxed than he had seen her in a long time, and she had mentioned this afternoon that she finally had her operation under control. They had "broken the code" for handling Zoolandia paperwork procedures. Along with her new terminals had arrived several new workers. including a planning manager and a controller.

Charlie took another sip of his wine and smiled.

"Yes, things are finally smoothing out."

Mike arrived just in time to make a short speech after dinner. He didn't have a prepared speech.

"I won't go through all the things I said at the employee celebration because you all heard it then. I do want to say that I am especially proud of the job all of you have done. You are the ones who kept the chaos to a minimum, through excellent leadership and innovative problem-solving. Thank you very much, each and every one of you."

He stopped talking and stood looking out over the group. There was a sadness about him. The group began to feel uncomfortable. What was going on? Finally Mike continued.

"I hope you will all cherish the plaques you've received tonight. It's ironic that I chose plaques with the Zoolandia logo as a way of recognizing you. I had a call just a few minutes ago from Elliott Elephant. He has informed me that Zoolandia just divested itself of its theme park division."

The room gasped.

"I'll be damned," said Charlie.

"Here we go again."

Study Questions

Chapter 1
Overcommunication during an acquisition is almost impossible. Employees are fearful about their futures and want any kind of news. Rumors, which usually forecast dire consequences, race through the organization. While open communication can't eliminate rumors entirely, it signals employees that they are valued, respected, and entitled to whatever information is available.

- What is your philosophy on sharing information with employees in your own organization on a continuing basis?
- How would your philosophy help or hinder you in times of tremendous change such as acquisition?

Cultures merge during any acquisition. In *Organizational Culture and Leadership,* Edgar Schien defines culture as a pattern of basic assumptions that have been accepted as valid to the point they are taken for granted. These assumptions become the deepest and most strongly held aspects of culture. They are manifested in the organization's structure, strategies, language, systems, stories and myths, and daily routines.

- How would you describe the Happy Valley and Zoolandia cultures from what you know so far?
- What do you perceive as the major difficulties in merging these two cultures and what steps would you take at this point to help smooth the transition?
- How is the culture of your own organization similar to the Happy Valley and Zoolandia cultures?

Chapter 2

William Bridges, in *Transitions: Making Sense of Life's Changes,* describes the transition process as having three stages: ending, neutral zone, and beginning. Every beginning is preceded by a difficult ending, a painful stage of the transition.

- Happy Valley animals are faced with the ending of the zoo as they have known it, and they react strongly in ways that are different from the ways they have acted in the past. What behaviors and feelings seem to be new or different?
- What behaviors and feelings in your organization have been manifested at the "ending stage" of a major change?

When an acquisition moves to the neutral zone, "old ways" are abolished and "new ways" not yet established. In this time of chaos, employees rely on their own skills and strengths to cope.

- What coping skills (positive and negative) do the Happy Valley animals use, and what impact does the animals' behavior have on the operation of the zoo?
- How do employees in your organization cope when they are in that ambiguous time of the neutral zone?

Chapter 3

The relationship between management and labor can be severely strained during an acquisition. Management must work with the unions to discuss and agree upon ways to handle contractual and transitional issues, to foster a spirit of cooperation, and to demonstrate recognition of labor's critical role in the success of the emerging company.

- What benefits might come from the meetings between the union and Charlie and Liz?
- What further steps would you take to gain union cooperation?
- What labor-management issues in your organization would be exacerbated by a dramatic change situation such as acquisition?

During acquisition, middle managers (trying to function as advocates, messengers, and decision-makers) may be caught between two or more constituencies with different goals and perspectives. Often middle managers must represent upper management to the workers and vice versa.

- How does this dynamic play out at Happy Valley? Which managers experience the most conflict between constituencies?
- What survival strategies do you use when you must act as the go-between for two constituencies in your organization?

Chapter 4

The human resources aspect of an acquisition most often determines whether an acquisition fails or succeeds, yet more attention usually is paid to its fiscally strategic aspects. A balance of focus will ease the transition.

- What indications are there in the story that sufficient attention is/is not being paid to the workers' needs during the acquisition?
- What measures are used in your organization to monitor the human element during change? Suggest corrective measures.

When two organizations merge, managers find it difficult to determine the degree of discretion they have regarding policies and procedures in the new entity. This is particularly difficult when the acquired organization is small and informal and the acquiring organization is massive and standardized.

- How can employees, particularly in an acquired organization, determine the organization's norms about policies and procedures and about following the rules versus taking initiative?
- What is the balance between compliance and initiative in your organization, and how do you determine where to draw the line?

Chapter 5

Continued change and chaos have a cumulative effect on employees. This may trigger an eruption over what seems like a minor event, a consequence that acquisition managers may not anticipate because they cannot see the whole system, they have not thought through possible scenarios created by the change, and/or because a few people simply cannot think of everything. Sometimes unintended or unexpected outcomes are good, but to paraphrase the nursery rhyme, "when they are bad, they are very bad." And they are bad when they do not make sense, when they undermine management credibility, and when they create havoc with employees' sense of security.

- What unintended consequences of change occur at Zoolandia, and what response do these consequences trigger from employees?
- What might Zoolandia have done to minimize unintended consequences?
- What events might act as unintended triggers in your organization?

Chapter 6

Commonalties bring people into coalitions to work toward shared goals during times of change. Often these coalitions are made up of what in "normal" times would seem like unlikely combinations. To be successful during times of change, managers need to be able to drop old cultural filters and look at employees with new eyes, seeking skills and expertise to help accomplish tasks and reach goals.

- The Happy Valley animals successfully form coalitions to fight with Zoolandia management. List the coalitions and the commonalities that helped form them.
- What non-traditional coalitions could you bring together in your organization that would help you solve a problem or reach a goal?

Risk-taking is a course of action or inaction taken under conditions exposing one to possible loss in order to reach a desired outcome. During times of great change, playing it safe by taking no action can be of higher risk than taking action. Employees expect commitment.

- Assess the risk Charlie Fox takes in his shift from trying to please both management and labor to becoming an advocate for labor? What are the risks for each stance?
- How is risk valued or punished in your organization? How would this approach to risk help/hurt your organization during times of drastic change?

Chapter 7

The last transitional stage in William Bridges' theory is the beginning stage following the neutral zone. In this fragile stage, employees are still integrating new ways of being and will not be highly productive.

To get through this stage successfully, managers must allow extra time in schedules and provide encouragement and support to the workers.

- What is management's expectation of the workers when Theme Park 46 opens its doors?
- What support might managers give the workers as they struggled to learn their jobs while handling a high volume of new customers?
- What provisions are made in your organization to provide extra support for employees experiencing drastic change?

Celebrations and rites of passages give managers the opportunity to show appreciation for and recognize employees' efforts and progress during drastic change.

- The well-received Zoolandia Theme Park 46 employee celebration visibly raises the level or morale. Is the timing of the celebration as effective as it might be?
- What would be your approach to recognizing employee efforts at the zoo?
- What forms of recognition are used and what behaviors are recognized in your organization? How would this approach help or hinder a major change process?

The Dynamics of Corporate Culture

What is culture?
Culture has the properties of glue, bonding a collection of people into a group. When people come together to form a group they establish guidelines by deciding what they want to accomplish and how they are going to do it. These guidelines reflect the values of the group, which are reinforced as its members work together, learn from experience, and build relationships. Over time, a collection of beliefs and assumptions evolves from continued success; these become the foundation of the group culture, accepted and integrated to the point of being taken for granted as the way to view the world.

In recent years a science similar to that of anthropology, the study of man as both animal and member of society, has been used to study and diagnose organizational cultures. This "organizational anthropology" studies visible day-to-day behaviors and artifacts and attaches cultural meanings to them. The areas usually examined for cultural meaning include these:

The *mission* of an organization is stated in terms of its purpose for existing and its position in the marketplace. Why is this company unique and what does it provide that other companies do not? The mission statement may also include the organization's philosophy on such things as technology, competition, treatment of employees and customers, and social responsibility. Company slogans such as "We try harder" or "The employee-owned company" try to capture the essence of the company mission.

The *structure* of an organization reflects how work is divided, how decisions are made, and how power is distributed, as well as basic philosophy about how workers are to be managed. A hierarchical structure with layers of management uses positional authority and formal reporting relationships to direct employees, who aren't trusted to make decisions. This type of structure is more common in the traditional organization, particularly that with a high degree of specialization. A more organic structure in which self-managed work groups are trusted and empowered to make job-related decisions is becoming more common today. Fewer management layers and the redefinition of management's mission to serve the first-line worker by removing obstacles to performance are characteristic of the organic structure.

A *common language* unique to the group culture gives members a sense of identity. Only insiders know the meaning of the vocabulary, which may include technical jargon, acronyms, slogans, gestures, nicknames, and shorthand phrases. The language gives many clues to cultural beliefs. For example, sports metaphors such as "step up to the plate" and "take the ball and run with it" or military metaphors such as "a good soldier" or "he's like a Sherman tank" may reflect a competitive male culture. In an organization that is resting on its laurels or resisting change, expressions like "if it ain't broke, don't fix it" or "you can't argue with success" are common.

The *reward system* defines desirable behaviors, how those behaviors are reinforced, and how status is acquired. An informal reward system can prove more powerful than a formal one, such as when a company formally espouses quality by naming an "employee of the month" for meeting all aspects of a contract but quietly gives a raise to the employee who saves money by "cutting corners" even to the detriment of a product.

The organization reinforces beliefs and assumptions about leaders and events through its *myths and stories*. These often tend to make leaders look larger than life, people who can be trusted to beat any odds. Employees also develop stories and myths reflecting their beliefs and assumptions. In organizations with adversarial relationships between labor and management, labor may have stories about heroes who outwit or triumph over management. Humorous stories and jokes, often targeting those not trusted because of their membership in management, ethnic, social, or political groups, are used to build a sense of camaraderie, to dispel worries, diffuse tension, or make intolerable situations more tolerable.

Subcultures are smaller groups within a larger culture group. They are made up of people who share some particular values that are different from those of other groups within the corporation. Membership may be determined by such things as department or division, occupation or profession, or project team. The forming of subcultures is normal; it can give members a more intimate sense of belonging. As long as an organizational culture is strong enough to bind together and integrate its subcultures, subcultures pose no problem to the organization. But if the organizational culture is weak, rivalry between subcultures (such as competition for resources between a research group that wants to develop new products and a manufacturing group that wants to increase production of existing products) may pull it in several directions and create chaos.

Subcultures whose values conflict with organizational culture are *countercultures*. Rank-and-file workers may bond together, for instance, because they believe the organization's values are tied to profit-and-loss statements to the exclusion of the interests of the worker. Countercultures may also form to undermine targeted authorities or groups who are perceived as enemies or competitors.

Cultural evolution

For further definition of a particular corporate culture, consider the organization's relationship with its environment, that is, the information it takes in, what it disregards, and what action results.

Organizational cultures go through stages—from formation to stability to maturity. In the formation stage, environment is a major factor in dictating the basic mission and division of labor. In a mature and stable culture, beliefs and assumptions act as filters, regulating the flow of information from the environment. By screening out irrelevant information, the filters help reduce the amount of information requiring attention to a manageable size.

At the same time, a company that has enjoyed success and wants to maintain the status quo may inadvertently filter out important messages about dangers and opportunities, thus limiting its response to a changing environment. Ken Olson, president of Digital Equipment Corporation, said in 1977, "There is no reason for any individual to have a computer in their home," preventing the company from capitalizing on the explosive personal computer market. Happy Valley Zoo's cultural filters keep it from seeing the trend toward high-tech theme parks, and it continues business without innovation, assuming customers will continue as usual too.

Cultural filters often influence hiring practices, serving to screen out people whose values don't align with the organizational culture. The advantage of this practice is the comfort of familiarity; its disadvantage is a lack of diversity among employees and the potential for "group think," that is, pressure to conform and to support group decisions even when a member believes it to be wrong. This phenomenon is the motivation behind many bad business decisions such as continuing unsuccessful products, ignoring problems, and dismissing innovative ideas.

All of the areas and dynamics (internal and external) of an organization so far discussed give clues to the underlying culture of an organization, but they must be interpreted as a whole to paint a clear cultural picture, and interpretation is always tainted by the interpreter's personal perceptions and biases. Use such interpretation to establish a hypothesis that can be examined, accepted, corrected, or rejected as new information surfaces. Then use your diagnoses and hypotheses to help decide when and how to introduce change.

Cultures during mergers and acquisitions
Change efforts often fail because organizations persistently ignore the human need to hold onto the familiar and avoid the unknown. This is most dramatic in mergers or acquisitions in which entire companies are swallowed up as if they never existed. But the old companies continue to exist in the hearts and minds of acquired employees. They cling to the culture that once gave meaning to their lives as they try to survive the chaos of change. Employees who are told (in whatever way) that their culture is no longer valid and must be discarded will feel that they are not valid and they too will be discarded. This dynamic creates an urgency to end the chaos of a cultural void and of two cultures competing for survival. Such conditions prevent employees from focusing on the tasks to be done, and productivity plummets.

A new culture, the glue that bonds, cannot be built overnight but evolves over a long period of time. Successful companies, however, don't let the new culture simply evolve in just any way; they craft it to support the organization's vision and strategy based on the reality of the environment. The process of crafting takes into consideration the beliefs and assumptions that form the current cultures of both organizations. On one hand, it reinforces the beliefs and assumptions that support the new vision and strategy. On the other, it works to eliminate obsolete beliefs and assumptions—not an easy process and one that can't be rushed. Obsolete beliefs and assumptions must first be raised to the conscious level of the employee groups. The next step is to help employees let go of old beliefs by providing a vision of what the organization is striving to be—strategically and culturally. The greater the difference between the old and new culture, the greater the resistance by employees and the longer the process.

The most important factor in minimizing chaos is a strong and visible leader who provides a vision that both acquiring and acquired employee groups can understand and support. The leader can also instill trust in the employees that s/he is able to lead the new corporation through ambiguity to a promising future. The leader must be impartial in dealing with both employee groups, eliciting the talents of all employees and supporting desired cultural norms from both sides to avoid the "us vs. them" dynamic.

Patience and consistency are virtues in this process: patience because cultural changes are evolutionary and, though they can be crafted to fit strategy, they can't be rushed; consistency because employees quickly pick up discrepancies. Management must model the beliefs and behaviors it wants from employees. However long it takes, a culture supporting the corporate vision and strategy, allowing meaningful dialogue between management and employees, and involving employees in the crafting of the future, is worth the effort.—CF

Breaking the "Us vs. Them" Barrier

Mergers and acquisitions represent the greatest challenges for labor relations professionals. This is true whether they work for the acquiring or acquired company, whether they represent management or labor. The transition period involved in any merger or acquisition causes every employee to experience fear and insecurity. Labor relations professionals, who are also employees, are not immune. In fact, their feelings are often intensified or distorted by their daily immersion in the anxieties of others, which become the very substance of their work.

No matter how experienced or educated they may be, labor relations professionals are handicapped by the almost uncontrollable polarization occurring during an acquisition. The union representative for workers of an acquiring company, for example, is instantly juxtaposed against two different management groups and simultaneously squared off against union workers at the acquired company. Similarly, the manager of labor relations at the acquiring company must contend with twice as many unions and must interact with the manager of labor relations from the acquired company.

In addition, these professionals must cope with the constantly changing and evolving responses of both management and labor to the merger or acquisition process. These responses not only break down the traditional lines of communication between management and labor but also assault the fundamental nature of the relationship.[1] In this environment, the successful labor relations professional must be able to compartmentalize his or her own fears and insecurities and bring a flexible, creative, and calm maturity to the process. This means recognizing that there must be no winners and losers in a merger, that acquired employees have feelings of powerlessness, and that fears, including his or her own, must be conquered. This requires a constant self-checking process through which one identifies, analyzes, and sorts out feelings of one's own to separate them from the general task of representing others.

Too often the acquisition process is viewed as one in which labor must be managed or "dealt with."[2] This is no more true than a belief that management must be "dealt with." The undeniable fact is that all parties (generally two managements and two labor groups[3]) need each other in more than a superficial "dealing" way. The organizational health and profitability of the surviving entity depends to a great extent on the ability of the employees in all four groups to cooperate in the continuation of the business. Likewise, the continued employment of some or all of the employees in all four groups depends on the organization's financial well-being. Like it or not, the various groups need each other.

No Winners or Losers
The first step toward the conclusion of a successful transaction involves recognition that no one benefits if there is a perceived winner or loser in the labor relations arena. This does not mean individuals are not harmed, but that it is a mistake to project, directly or indirectly, that the employees of the acquired company are less worthy or less skilled than those of the acquiring firm because their organization has been "taken over" or "conquered." Employees who receive this message, whether management or labor, harbor resentments and hostilities that can last not only for the duration of the transition but for the entire length of their careers. The mildest manifestation of this resentment is a simple but costly lack of respect; the most extreme is industrial sabotage.

The burden of obligation falls more heavily on the labor relations professionals of the acquiring entity because they have more control. They can set the tone, creating an organizational environment that is welcoming rather than hostile. Enlightened consciousness does not come naturally. It requires self-evaluation to ensure honest acceptance that all employees involved in the transaction are equal. It further requires a conscious program of both direct and indirect messages that there are no winners or losers in the process.

A lesser but still significant responsibility falls on their labor relations counterparts in the acquired company—a cooperative effort to actively homogenize the workforce. It demands restraint in focusing on errors made by the acquiring company that inadvertently demean the acquired workforce. It suggests an active role in quelling rather than whipping up hysteria, and it abhors playing the victim.

To promote fear and discontent by hypothesizing problems that do not exist (whether through open acrimony in union publications or casual whispers during coffee breaks) is counter to the best interests of the employees and the organization. Employees companywide believe, and reasonably so, that the labor relations managers and union representatives of both companies are privy to data concerning the future of the workforce. When these professionals allow their own fears and worries to interfere with their representational obligations, they risk breaching the trust of their position and cause unnecessary distress to the very people they are charged to protect.

Feelings of Powerlessness and Fear
In their private lives, workers have enormous discretion over financial, spiritual, social, and political matters, and they feel competent to make decisions about them. Workers usually experience a lesser degree of personal power at work since their sphere of influence is often limited to a small, defined area. During merger or acquisition, an acquired worker's power is often abrogated to his or her counterpart in the acquiring company. And even when this is not the case, the worker may perceive it to be true or fear it to be inevitable.

When the mind perceives danger, a coordinated symphony of events results in what has been called the "fight-or-flight response." People perceiving danger, even where there is none, react not so much to reality as to their internal associations based on past experience. They worry about what will happen tomorrow, what the future will bring, how long they will live, how they will pay their bills, and whether there will be a nuclear war.[4] Overshadowing all other worries during mergers is the concern about whether they will continue to have a job. Second to that is whether they will lose pay, status, rank, responsibility, or seniority. All these worries result in low morale and decreased productivity.

This is not to say that all such fears are baseless. Since most companies do not need a duplicate set of managers in any department, the likelihood that jobs, including labor relations jobs, will be eliminated and managers laid off is great. Managers usually have little or no protection. Their fear of termination has a basis in reality and must be addressed quickly and in a positive fashion.

Those in the ranks of labor have an equally legitimate fear of layoff, though an organized process governed by contract and applicable law usually helps join the workforces and distribute the work. Inherent in these processes is the natural tendency for each side to perceive a winner and a loser. No matter how impartial the application of the process, no matter how well-intentioned the participants, the process almost always results in both groups seeing themselves as the loser, and both seeing the other as the winner. Only when the parties take decision-making into their own hands and management stays completely out of it are the results anything other than unsatisfying to everyone.

The challenges to labor relations professionals in all parties to a merger are equal:
- to accept acquired workers as valuable assets, not treat them as if they were failures because of their situation
- to compartmentalize their own fears and anxieties, to keep them separate from organizational responsibilities
- to minimize negative reactions resulting from the stress of the situation through responsible dissemination of accurate information that is, to the greatest extent possible, non-inflammatory.

If all parties to a merging transaction act in accordance with the charges above, general detente is not hard to imagine. When employees from an acquiring company treat those from an acquired firm as valuable, the acquired employees have less fear and, as a result, experience less stress. Employees with less stress are less likely to imagine baseless threats and are better-equipped to deal with the real consequences of change. When all employees feel more secure and less threatened, the organization as a whole can successfully address the needs of everyone and minimize transition trauma and loss.

The events described in *Someone Is Buying the Zoo* illustrate the each of these problems. Charlie Fox, for example, as the embodiment of the management labor relations professional in the acquired company, struggling with his own insecurities as he interacts with the union in his professional role. Is his effectiveness compromised by his personal feelings? Liz Lioness, the labor relations professional from Zoolandia, the acquiring company, has a different reaction and approach. She does not feel insecure but in control. Does she exercise her control responsibly?

During the acquisition process at Happy Valley Zoo, the animals become more fearful and less empowered. Zoolandia creates this situation both actively and passively. The effect of Zoolandia's actions even leads to sabotage. What active steps by Zoolandia engender fear and resentment in the employees? Are the goals of those actions appropriate or inappropriate? If the goals are appropriate, how might they be served in a more constructive and healthy way?

What passive or inadvertent actions on Zoolandia's part contribute to Happy Valley animals' feelings of powerlessness and fear? How might companies learn to identify when they are about to make an inadvertent error in this area?

Unlike what takes place in the Happy Valley story, labor relations issues that naturally arise during mergers or acquisitions should be on the transition agenda from the very beginning. Guidance as to the correct handling of such issues must come directly from the top of the organization and must be carried out with chief executive authority. When transition personnel are left to their own devices to determine the course, the result can be a self-serving hodge-podge. The mandate for an appropriate labor relations policy in the merger environment is good social policy as well as good business.—CS

---

[1] In "Trade Unions and Takeovers: Labor's Response to Mergers and Acquisitions," *Human Resource Planning* 12 (2): 167-77, Hoyt N. Wheeler chronicles the changing response of unions to such transactions. He cites collective bargaining, litigation, corporate ownership strategies, and takeover legislation.

[2] See B. J. Leukart, "Dealing with Labor When a Company Is Sold," *Mergers and Acquisitions,* 19 (1) (Spring 1984): 40-44.

[3] In fact, there may be many more than four parties, including multiple unions with varying interests, or multiple managements.

[4] Loren W. Harrington, quoting Joan Borysenko, M.D., a Harvard Medical School instructor and director of the Mind/Body Group Programs for the Division of Behavioral Medicine at Beth Israel Hospital, Boston, in "Stress," *Air Line Pilot Magazine,* 55 (8): 27-49.

The Human Processes of Change

Change of any kind is difficult for organizations, and acquisition is among the most traumatic. The impact of acquisition is more intense than other changes because it challenges everything employees believe to be stable and because the secrecy surrounding most acquisitions encourages their feelings of powerlessness and confusion.

Most often acquisition is the considered decision of only a few people, affecting a whole employee population that has had no voice in the decision. Even when acquisition is the only viable economic choice and clearly in the best interests of the enterprise, to affected employees the cure can seem worse than the disease. Consequently, an understanding of the dynamics of change is essential to the successful management of acquisition.

The easiest way to examine change dynamics is from the individual's perspective. Individuals look for meaning and order in the world and when they find it, they feel secure. This order and meaning provides a sense of how life is constructed and how elements of the world relate to each other. In the workplace, this meaning and order provides an understanding of how work gets done and how employee contributions fit into a larger scheme.

Each person sees and interprets differently, but most hold common the belief that there is some basic order that allows individuals to anticipate what will come next in their lives. With this construct plus personal experience, each person creates the unique story that is his or her life, complete with meaning and order. This is the work of a lifetime.

Individual stories overlap in larger systems of families, friends, and co-workers. Stories depend on each other and affect each other at the points where they intersect. In the overlaps, values are explored, experiences are shared, and mutual purposes emerge. Through this (admittedly simplified) basic process each person develops a unique being in the world, simultaneously inventing him or herself and growing an awareness of how each fits with others in a larger society.

This process is played out in the workplace with the addition of technical and economic systems to structure and direct productive work. Workplace systems form around a purpose and meaning that are explicitly stated or demonstrated in the way people work together and what they produce. All the systems working together are an organization, an aggregate entity that considers its own questions of fit and writes its own story. Once created, the organization's story is part of every individual who is part of the organization. Change the organization story and individual stories change too.

The organization is a complex structure that spends much of its energy maintaining its own stability. It can be thought of as a hologram, where the whole is reflected in each of the parts and change to any part results in change to the whole. Given that both the parts and the whole of an organization are made up of human beings who prize order, meaning, and stability, the resistance to change is not surprising.

Nature usually gives us change in very small doses. Animals, plants, and people evolve slowly, probably because humankind would otherwise be thrown into a panic. Routine, incremental change is absorbed as a matter of course and barely noticed. But such evolution is not the only kind affecting people or their organizations. People experience discontinuous change just as does nature in its lightning and earthquakes. There are interrupts in the flow, abrupt reversals, and broad upheavals.

Abrupt change is profoundly unsettling. The more significant or unexpected the change, the harder it is for individuals and organizations to accept and integrate the change and move on. Acquisitions consist of "mega" discontinuous changes; they interrupt predictable patterns and introduce frightening uncertainty. Organizations can be literally scared stiff. Frightened into immobility by discontinuous change, employees even become unable to resume patterns of evolutionary change. Suddenly no change is safe, and the organization becomes immobile too.

Organizational changes like acquisition often fail because management believes change will occur simply because it is economically sensible or because a detailed plan outlines exactly what employees are expected to do. Management usually adds a few other requirements. Change must be cost-efficient and fast, with minimum impact on productivity. Unfortunately, management intent alone cannot overcome organizational immobility or individual fear and resistance.

Change may be planned with an end state in mind and steps are laid out to accomplish the end state in an orderly fashion, but that is not all there is to it. The acquisition of Happy Valley Zoo (HVZ), for example, requires the computerization of the HVZ accounting office using the Zoolandia system. The goal of an automated office is clear, and the steps to accomplish the goal emerge quickly. On paper, the straightforward changes work well. With employees, however, the process becomes chaos. Work doubles as employees support both old and new systems, communication is short-circuited, and the department manager goes to pieces. This reasonable change is only one small increment of an acquisition. It needn't generate such turmoil, but it does.

The hologram metaphor is useful in examining the process of change. Changing one part changes all parts, changing the whole as well. Every change in every department is felt to some degree by everyone in the organization. The accounting office feels pressure from its own changes as well as from every other change happening across the organization. And because of the acquisition, there are many changes occurring simultaneously. The aggregate pressure overwhelms the workers and their manager. In the same way that a hologram cannot be captured in one dimension, the climate of acquisition and change affecting many people cannot be understood or managed from a single perspective.

William Bridges provides a helpful explanation in his book *Transitions*. People "transition" from old to new. They must first let go of the old way, something that is hard to do because regret about losing the familiar is so powerful. Once letting-go begins, a time warp or suspension, during which they are not entirely out of the old or all the way into the new, occurs. Somewhere in between, they enter what Bridges calls a "neutral zone," in which people are confused and overwhelmed by the ambiguity of being in two places at once. They may feel lost and empty, and they are not very productive. They can even get stuck in this adjustment phase, unable to find the commitment or initiative required to move toward the new goals.

Employees in the neutral zone are processing both the old and new scenarios. The change from old to new interrupts the personal storyline, forcing a new plot and new conclusions that can undermine some very basic assumptions individuals hold about themselves. Rewriting their personal stories raises identity questions as well as fears about loss of control. In the neutral zone, individuals ask, "Who am I now that my story is changing? Am I the same person I was? What is expected of me? How will I be useful?"

Organizations and individuals often hold the mistaken belief that change must be remedial, that the organization wouldn't need fixing if it weren't broken. "If we were doing everything right, change wouldn't be necessary," they say. This belief evokes questions about meaning and the quality of a person's contribution to the organization. Issues involving belonging and the future also surface as the individual questions the potential loss of relationships associated with old ways or becomes confused about how to fit in with the new.

In the neutral zone, painful personal questions manifest in every employee affected by the organization change. Pain becomes more intense during acquisition because changes are sweeping and individuals have little input and little information about how the organizational story is rewritten. Anxiety about change manifests in a variety of forms. Some people try to "freeze-frame," not letting go of the past. Others rush to implement the new before they understand it, trying to appear enthusiastic regardless of how they feel. Employees may become angry or depressed; they may withdraw or pick fights, gripe or gossip. Because anxiety and resistance can take so many forms, management may not recognize them and assume that all is well.

A safer assumption is that anxiety and resistance are present and must be worked through by each employee according to a very personal clock. The pace of change in an organization is subject to its many individual clocks, and implementation of desired changes is possible only when everyone is ready. In the mean time, previously efficient operations may become erratic as systemwide absenteeism increases, productivity declines, and communication, no matter how carefully planned, goes haywire.

Personal and systemwide responses to change usually present an unappealing picture and a significant challenge to managers. The question arises: "Can acquisition ever be managed successfully?" Maybe, but there is no single method or recipe for success. Zoolandia, with its broad acquisition experience, believes it can cookie-cut little Zoolandias out of acquired facilities. But response to change and acquisition is so intensely personal for employees that no single plan can anticipate all the variables. The only really effective tools corporations have for acquisition are the sensitivity and good judgment of management personnel. Unfortunately, these qualities cannot be trained into managers as part of the acquisition process. Management skills must be in place before major change occurs.

During acquisition, managers must be attuned to the uncertainty and pain introduced by the prospect of change, understanding that employees are not infinitely adaptable. They must have both feet planted firmly in reality, asking, "What needs to be done? What is a workable time frame in which to do it? How can employees be involved and supported? How can management get good data and stay in touch throughout the process?" The answers to these questions will help competent managers exercise good judgment and prevent them from drifting off into confusion themselves.

Successful managers—empowered, competent, and sensitive managers who can stay focused and responsive during the turbulence natural to acquisition—are the key to successful acquisition. Managers at all levels must remember that change and acquisition are human endeavors whose success depends to a much greater degree on people than on economic or technical viability.—CG

Suggestions

Someone is Buying the Zoo tells the story of the animals in a small organization going through the painful process of acquisition by a large, impersonal conglomerate. The animals' reactions are dictated by their own perceptions about their circumstances and their ability to cope with change and uncertainty. The patterns of employee reaction to change are somewhat predictable according to a variety of theories. These theories give management a place to start in understanding and managing employee reactions during change. They give employees a place to start in understanding their feelings and learning to cope.

Mergers and acquisitions are unique in that they precipitate drastic change in a concentrated period of time. The greater and more rapid the change, the stronger employee reaction is likely to be. Managers can effectively use change theories to define strategy so long as they understand that each circumstance and every employee is unique. Because of this uniqueness, there are no shortcuts or quick fixes for the effective management of human resources during mergers and acquisitions; it is a time-consuming and intense process. Surprises are certain no matter how well change is planned.

Management implicitly or explicitly chooses one of two strategies: prevention or healing. The prevention strategy anticipates and makes accommodation for problems in advance to prevent damage. Those who say this slows the change process too much often find themselves taking even more time later to correct problems along the way. Unlike the prevention strategy, the after-the-fact strategy of healing something later, often leaves permanent scars. Prevention is a proactive strategy while healing is reactive.

The following change management suggestions can be used as a framework for building a personalized preventive strategy. This preventive process ideally begins long in advance of the change event, though realistically there may not be the luxury of a long lead time.

The executive staffs of both acquiring and acquired organizations play a central role in the merger or acquisition process while maintaining the day-to-day management of business to assure continuity and stability. The executive staffs of both companies begin the process by issuing a formal statement of organizational philosophy, creed, and charter as well as a statement emphasizing their support of the vision and goal of the change initiative. During the entire change process, members of the executive staffs are visible to employees in modeling desired behavior and alignment between beliefs and behavior. (Employees become cynical when they perceive management behavior suggesting "Do as we say, not as we do.")

The executive staff appoints key people, relieving them of functional duties, to serve on a Human Resource Transition Steering Committee (HRTSC), whose mission is to manage the change initiative as similar departments from the two organizations are melded. The HRTSC is comprised of management representatives of both organizations (acquiror and acquiree) as well as a human resource and a labor representative from each. Management members are selected for their organizational/technical expertise and knowledge and their organizational position. Labor members are selected by labor for the same basic reasons. Management does not interfere with labor's selections.

The HRTSC operates in an advisory capacity to the executive staff, which makes final decisions. Once decisions are made, the HRTSC has chairman's authority to implement them—directly or by delegation to a task force under its direction. If a task force is used, its members are carefully selected to include functionaries and representatives from all relevant constituencies. Ideally, the HRTSC involves as many people as possible to provide a sense of control. Change is perceived as a threat when done *to* the people and as an opportunity when done *by* the people affected.

The HRTSC is empowered to address these areas:

Effective **communication** does not make problems disappear but it helps minimize them, reducing the "worry factor" (employee concern about "what will happen to me?"). In the early stages of acquisition, an information vacuum, partly due to legal obligations, often occurs. Employees spend more time trying to get information and understand what is happening and less time on productive work. A more open communications process can provide this information, allowing peace of mind and the return or worker attention to productivity.

The mission of the HRTSC is to find and use a variety of mechanisms for moving information into the organization. Effective strategies might include:
- Designating specific internal and external spokespersons, to minimize the problem of mixed or multiple messages
- Advising all employees of the names and sources of official information
- Training all spokespersons, particularly as to the importance of disseminating accurate, authorized information
- Communicating clearly and often, telling as much as you can as soon as you can
- Developing empathic, non-defensive feedback mechanisms for management and the employees, so that questions and concerns can be shared, support can be elicited and offered
- Using diverse communication forums such as regular and special newsletters, focus groups, telephone hotlines, videotapes, and large group presentations

Culture definition and integration helps employees understand and begin to accept a new pattern of beliefs and assumptions for the new organization. Combining two very different organizations can create a culture clash of "us versus them," in which each group stereotypes the other. Handle the merging of cultures with great care.

The mission of the HRTSC is to integrate cultures, retaining the best of each. Use strategies such as:
- Analyzing the cultures of each organization to identify areas of commonality and areas for potential clash
- Validating the good in each culture without weighing in favor of the acquiring culture (avoid negative, derogatory, or deprecating labeling of the acquired culture)
- Developing a formal plan for merging cultures that incorporates the best of each one
- Planing high-visibility events such as rites of passage and celebrations for letting go of both previous cultures and accepting the new combined one
- Inventing new traditions, rites, and celebrations to replace the old and to be shared by all employees in the new culture
- Distributing a glossary of terms and jargon so that both groups speak the language

A formal **labor relations policy** is necessary in a status quo environment, critical in a merging environment. A formal policy reduces the adversarial atmosphere by exhibiting a formal commitment to management's relationship with all employees and reduces hostilities between and among competing employee groups and unions.

The mission of the HRTSC, whose members include labor relations professionals, is to oversee the development of a written labor relations policy, to address the unique circumstances of the merger, to identify problem areas, and to solve problems with the involved employee groups and unions, effecting a cooperative transition. Effective strategies include:

- Developing a written labor relations policy that addresses the *common elements* (commitment to the laws and regulations governing the employment relationship, to the spirit and intent as well as to the words of any collective bargaining agreements, to a grievance or redress procedure for employees who do not have one by virtue of contract, to a meaningful process whereby employees can make suggestions and improvements, and to the best possible working conditions that the contract and/or relationship allow) and *merger-specific elements* (commitment to treat employees from each company fairly and without partiality, to allow the internal process of the labor organizations to follow their prescribed course without interference, and to support and accept mutually agreed-upon or mandated results of the union processes) of such a contract
- Minimizing disparate treatment of employees from the two companies (standardize rates of pay, hours of service, and working conditions for similarly situated employees)
- Encouraging employee and union input on task forces established to identify problems and suggest resolutions

For effective integration, **systems and procedures,** the most visible part of life in any organization (daily, weekly, monthly, quarterly, and annual cycles of routines, procedures, reports, forms, and other recurrent tasks) must have a common database and set of criteria.

The HRTSC's mission is to synthesize multiple systems into one meeting the needs of the new organization. Effective strategies include:

- Developing a single, consistent reward system (except as already negotiated in labor agreements) that reflects organizational values and priorities by rewarding and correcting particular behaviors and designating how promotion is achieved. Include discussion of performance appraisal and compensation (bonuses, perquisites, and benefits such as tuition reimbursement).
- Developing a training system that helps employees understand change and how it affects them, helps affected employees replan

their worklives, provides employee change management skills, and gives managers skills for handling their own change while managing change for others. Include but do not limit the program to classroom training.
- Replacing pre-existing programs with a new, confidential Employee Assistance Program run by counseling professionals with acquisition experience. Times of change can heighten or aggravate pre-existing but undiscovered chemical dependency, marital, emotional, and other problems. Such counselors can help workers adjust to change and carry out their assignments. Make this service available to all employees and managers from both companies.

Evaluation of the change process is the final phase of change management. This phase has been reached when all task force and HRTSC initiatives have been taken, and their projects have been turned over to day-to-day operations. The HRTSC evolves from a temporary, full-time, transitional team to a permanent, part-time Human Resource Committee (HRC). The mission of the HRC is to evaluate the change initiative, prescribe correction, and recommend additional action as a continuing process. Effective strategies include:
- Evaluating the change process to make future transitions easier. Determine whether each aspect of the change procedure helped or hindered the process. Human resource impact studies might include productivity levels, stress-related disabilities, transfer and termination activity, thefts, and sabotage. Plot items in a timeline to identify patterns and connections with change events.
- Continuous monitoring of the effectiveness of the change process. Identify trouble spots through regular measurement of items addressed in the evaluation, and present them for consideration by the HRC. Other tools include regular employee satisfaction surveys, focus group meetings, and suggestion programs. Remember that feedback to employees is critical to their continued involvement. Solicit their suggestions and participation in planning for improvement. Make the HRC's attention to human resource issues a cultural norm, giving employees a clear signal that their needs, concerns, and contributions are important.

By using this concept of change management, organizations can minimize the pain of drastic change and have in place a vehicle for the effective management of future change. As Alvin Toffler said, "We must create an environment in which people want to cooperate with each other and it is in their interest to do so."

Bibliography

Adams, John D., ed. *Transforming Work.* Alexandria, Virginia: Miles River Press, 1984.

Bernstein, Aaron. *Grounded: Frank Lorenzo and the Destruction of Eastern Airlines.* New York: Simon and Schuster, 1990.

Bridges, William. *Transitions: Making Sense of Life's Changes.* Reading, Massachusetts: Addison-Wesley Publishing Company, 1980.

Brooks, John. *The Takeover Game: The Men, the Moves, and the Wall Street Money Behind Today's Nationwide Merger Wars.* New York: Truman Talley Books, 1987.

Buona, Anthony F., and James L. Bowditch. *The Human Side of Mergers and Acquisitions: Managing Collisions Between People, Cultures and Organizations.* San Francisco: Jossey-Bass, 1989.

Connor, Patrick E., and Linda Lake. *Managing Organizational Change.* New York: Praeger, 1988.

Deal, Terrence E., and Allen A. Kennedy. *Corporate Cultures: The Rites and Rituals of Corporate Life.* Reading, Massachusetts: Addison-Wesley Publishing Company, Inc., 1982.

Feldman, Steven P. "Stories as Cultural Creativity: On the Relation Between Symbolism and Politics in Organizational Change." *Human Relations* 43 (9): 809-28.

Geber, Beverly. "The Forgotten Factor in Merger Mania." *Training* (February 1987): 28-37.

Gleick, James. *Chaos: Making a New Science.* New York: Penguin Books, 1987.

Hallett, Jeffrey. *Worklife Visions: Redefining Work for the Information Economy.* Alexandria, Virginia: American Society for Personnel Administration, 1987.

Harrington, Loren W. "Stress." *Air Line Pilot Magazine,* 55 (8): 27-49.
Hirschhorn, Larry, and Thomas N. Gilmore. "The Psychodynamics of a Cultural Change: Learnings from a Factory." *Human Resource Management* (Summer 1989): 211-33.
Leukart, B.J. "Dealing with Labor When a Company Is Sold." *Mergers and Acquisitions,* 19 (1): 40-44.
Lippitt, Gordon L., Peter Langseth, and Jack Mossop. *Implementing Organizational Change.* San Francisco: Jossey-Bass, 1985.
Napier, Nancy D. , Glen Simmons, and Kay Stratton. "Communication During a Merger: The Experience of Two Banks." *Human Resource Planning* 12 (2): 105-22.
Reimann, Bernard C., and Yoash Wiener. "Corporate Culture: Avoiding the Elitist Trap." *Horizons* (March-April 1988): 36-44.
Schein, Edgar H. *Organizational Culture and Leadership.* San Francisco: Jossey-Bass, 1986.
Scott, Cynthia D., and Dennis T. Joffee. *Managing Organizational Change: Leading Your Team Through Transition.* Los Altos, California: Crisp Publications, 1989.
Trice, Harrison M., and Janice M. Beyer. "Studying Organizational Cultures Through Rites and Ceremonials." *Academy of Management Review* 9 (1984): 653-69.
Vaill, Peter B. *Managing as a Performing Art.* San Francisco: Jossey-Bass, 1989.
Wheeler, Hoyt N. "Trade Unions and Takeovers: Labor's Response to Mergers and Acquisitions." *Human Resource Planning* 12 (2): 167-77.
Woodward, Harry. *Aftershock: Helping People Through Corporate Change.* New York: J. Wiley and Sons, 1987.
Zaleznik, Abraham. "The Mythological Structure of Organizations and Its Impact." *Human Resource Management* 28 (2): 267-77.

For further reading
Adams, John D., Ph.D., ed. *Transforming Leadership: From Vision to Results.* Alexandria, Virginia: Miles River Press, 1986.
Beckhard, Richard, and Reuben T. Harris. *Organizational Transitions: Managing Complex Change.* Reading, Massachusetts: Addison-Wesley Publishing Company, 1977.
Bridges, William. *Surviving Corporate Transition.* New York: Doubleday, 1988.
Byrd, Richard E. *A Guide to Personal Risk Taking.* New York: AMACOM, 1974.

Drucker, Peter. *Managing in Turbulent Times.* New York: Harper & Row, Publishers, 1980.

Hallett, Jeffrey J. *Worklife Visions.* Alexandria, Virginia: American Society for Personnel Administration, 1987.

Hussey, D. E., and M. J. Langham. *Corporate Planning: The Human Factor.* New York: Pergamon Press, 1980.

Kanter, Donald L., and Philip H. Mirvis. *The Cynical Americans: Living and Working in an Age of Discontent and Disillusion.* San Francisco: Jossey-Bass, 1989.

Kanter, Rosabeth Moss. *The Change Masters.* New York: Simon and Schuster, 1983.

Kanter, Rosabeth Moss, and Barry A. Stein, eds. *Life In Organizations.* New York: Basic Books, Inc., 1979.

Kilmann, Ralph, Teresa Joyce Covin, and Associates. *Corporate Transformation.* San Francisco: Jossey-Bass, 1988.

Kindler, Herbert S., Ph.D. *Risk Taking: A Guide for Decision Makers.* Ontario, Canada: Crisp Publications, 1990.

Kirkpatrick, Donald L. *How to Manage Change Effectively.* San Francisco: Jossey-Bass, 1985.

London, Manuel. *Change Agents: New Roles and Innovation Strategies for Human Resource Professionals.* San Francisco: Jossey-Bass, 1988.

Ludeman, Kate. *The Work Ethic: How to profit from the Changing Values of the New Work Force.* New York: Penguin Books, 1989.

Morgan, Gareth. *Images of Organization.* Beverly Hills: Sage Publications, 1986.

Natemeyer, Walter E., ed. *Classics of Organizational Behavior.* Oak Park, Illinois: Moore Publishing Company, Inc., 1978.

Selye, Hans, M.D. *The Stress of Life.* 2d ed. New York: McGraw-Hill, 1984.

Someone Is Buying the Zoo

Balancing Organization and Employee Needs
in Mergers and Acquisitions

Charlotte Frampton
Cynthia Surrisi
Carolyn Gallagher

Someone Is Buying the Zoo uses animal characters in a story about corporate acquisition. Readers make their own connections between animal characteristics and those of fellow workers under the stress of change. Discussion questions, change theory articles, and change management suggestions help readers construct their own approaches to change in their work and personal lives. To order additional copies:

Name _____
Company_____
Address_____
City_____ State _____ Zip _____
Daytime phone (   )_____
Please send me _____ copies of **Someone Is Buying the Zoo**
(ISBN 0-9628090-0-4) @ $9.95. Total: _____
Shipping & handling for first book: __2.50__
$.50 each additional: _____
Applicable sales tax (6% MN): _____
TOTAL AMOUNT: _____

Method of payment, in U.S. dollars only (check one):
_____ Check or Money order enclosed
_____ C.O.D.
_____ Purchase Order # _____

Send this order form to: mollyockett press
                            275 Cimarron Road
                            St. Paul, MN 55124
                            (612) 454-3738

Charlotte Frampton has over ten years of experience as an organization development consultant in high-tech manufacturing, health care, and nonprofit organizations. She is president of her firm, Paradigm Consultants, and her particular areas of expertise include the management of organizational change, interpersonal relations, group dynamics, problem-solving and strategic planning. She earned a Master of Science degree in Human Resource Development from the American University, Washington, D.C. She has completed several National Training Labs workshops and is a member of the Association for Psychological Type and OD Network.

Cynthia Surrisi has served as labor relations counsel for both management and labor through several acquisitions and mergers in the airline industry. Her experience includes the negotiation of merger transition agreements, contract integrations, and representation disputes, as well as employee and management consulting on the effect of labor relations in mergers. She earned a Bachelor of Arts degree from the University of North Dakota and a Juris Doctor degree from William Mitchell College of Law in St. Paul, Minnesota.

Carolyn Gallagher is an organizational development consultant and president of her own firm, Organization Innovations. Previously she was a manager and internal consultant for a high-tech manufacturing firm. Her areas of specialty include organization design, strategic planning, and service quality. She earned a Master of Business Administration degree from St. Thomas College (now the University of St. Thomas), St. Paul, and has a bachelor's degree in Industrial Relations. She has completed the NTL Organizational Development Consultant Training Track and is a member of the Association for Psychological Type and the OD Network.

Rev. Robert P. White
4300 Glumack Drive, LT **3167**
St. Paul, Minnesota
55111-3003